# DAYS OF DELUSION

*I remain as ever looking for the Lord Jesus Christ unto eternal life.*

*Wm Miller*

WILLIAM MILLER

# DAYS OF DELUSION

## A STRANGE BIT OF HISTORY

BY

CLARA ENDICOTT SEARS

WITH ILLUSTRATIONS

BOSTON AND NEW YORK

HOUGHTON MIFFLIN COMPANY

The Riverside Press Cambridge

1924

The Riverside Press
CAMBRIDGE · MASSACHUSETTS
PRINTED IN THE U.S.A.

# PREFACE

HAVING lived part of each year for many years in the very heart of what was once one of the most vital rural centres of the great excitement in 1843–44, when William Miller prophesied the coming end of the world; having had long conversations with many of the old people who live along the ridges overlooking the wide sweep of the Nashua Valley and listened to what they had to tell of days long past, and what they had heard from those of the generation before them; and having become deeply interested in the strange psychological influences that swayed thousands away from the beaten track of normal activities during those years of atmospheric disturbances and overwrought spiritual and mental emotions, it occurred to the author that there must be a good many still living, in various parts of the country, whose recollections would be of value, and that all these gathered together would bring before us at close range a vivid picture of one of the most peculiarly emotional and hysterical episodes in the ins and outs of our past history. Consequently the following "Notice" was inserted in the columns of many of the leading newspapers issued in the States where the delusion had its strongest foothold. It read as follows:

Has any reader of this paper any recollection of having heard parents or grandparents tell of the great religious excitement in 1843, the year that William Miller predicted the end of the world? Any anecdotes of that period, or any information however trivial will be gratefully received by

CLARA ENDICOTT SEARS.
Address, etc., etc.

The immediate response was proof of the interest now widely prevalent in preserving everything relating to bygone days, whether of concrete facts or mental states, that can help to interpret the times to which they belonged. Members of Historical Societies in various places suggested ways and means of acquiring material, and gave the names of persons who could give reliable information. This assistance, as well as a spontaneous response from many quarters from those who love to recall the past and hold it in tender memory, has enabled the author to turn her account of this strange bit of psychological history into more or less of a human document. No attempt has been made to unravel the various points of William Miller's doctrine. A few explanations regarding his prophecy have been necessary in order to make clear the reasons that started the wave of agitation, which, gaining headway, carried thousands of over-impressionable men and women out on to a sea of dreams and delusions. First and foremost of those carried out was William Miller himself — an honest and sincere man, held fast in the throes of a fixed idea.

Out of the great number of letters received, the author has quoted only from those giving personal recollections or recollections received directly from near relatives, and has made sure of the sources from which she has drawn. The dating of the letters varies from 1920 to 1923.

The rest of the book needs no explanation — it tells the tale through the testimony of the writings and various outside reminiscences of that day, and through data collected by the author during years of neighborly intercourse with many of the dear old people of Worcester and Middlesex Counties.

She has tried to write the book in such a way as to give of-
fence to none, and at the same time draw a truthful picture
of those hysterical days with the aid of the material acquired
by her through her appeal to the public.

The collection of original letters, many of which have in
them material which the author would have liked to use, but
which her limited space did not permit, will, after being
bound, find a niche in the library of the Society for the
Preservation of New England Antiquities in Boston.

CLARA ENDICOTT SEARS

HARVARD, MASSACHUSETTS

# ACKNOWLEDGMENTS

THE author desires to thank the following persons for sending or giving her personal or family anecdotes of the religious excitement of 1843–44:

Mr. Phineas Harrington, Groton, Mass.
Mrs. Ellen A. Barrows, Groton, Mass.
Mr. Charles H. Waitt, West Acton, Mass.
Mr. Henry Clare, New Bedford, Mass.
Mrs. Ellen G. S. Wood, Springfield, Mass.
Miss Helen Bartlett Hamill, Worcester, Mass.
Miss Mary E. Hurley, Clinton, Mass.
Mrs. C. W. Spring, Cambridge, Mass.
Mrs. W. P. Walton, Lynn, Mass.
Mr. Henry Kittredge, Lowell, Mass.
Mrs. Susan L. Harris, West Millbury, Mass.
Mr. F. Rodliff, Pigeon Cove, Mass.
Mrs. George R. Peabody, Fitchburg, Mass.
Mr. Charles E. Foster, Manchester, N.H.
Mrs. J. K. Turiot, Washington, D.C.
Mr. John Whitcomb, Lunenburg, Mass.
Mr. B. H. Savage, Townsend, Mass.
Miss Jane S. Hall, Washington County Historical Society, Pa.
Miss Ellen K. Stevens, Clinton, Mass.
Miss Annie Montague Winslow, Danvers, Mass.
Mr. H. T. Boyington, Prentiss, Maine.
Miss Helen Nescott Noyes, Lowell, Mass.
Mr. M. F. Plimpton, Fitchburg, Mass.
Mrs. Ellen M. Davenport, Worcester, Mass.
Mrs. W. S. Dudley, Harvard, Mass.
Miss Julia M. Warner, Philadelphia, Pa.
Mrs. M. J. Warner, Boylston Centre, Mass.
Mrs. George U. Lass, Worcester, Mass.
Miss Marion R. Sawyer, Rockville Centre, L.I.
Mrs. Hattie A. Robinson, Littleton Common, Mass.
Mrs. Delia E. Dalrymple, Millbury, Mass.
Mrs. J. K. Barker, Longmeadow, Mass.
Mr. Charles E. Keyser, Philadelphia, Pa.
Miss Laura Davis, Fitchburg, Mass.
Mrs. M. J. Taber, New Bedford, Mass.
Miss Eugenie J. Gibson, Woodsville, N.H.
Mrs. Thos. H. Berry, Philadelphia, Pa.
Mr. S. J. Marsh, Manchester, N.H.
Mrs. Estella Cone Fanning, Westfield, Mass.
Mrs. Horace T. Smith, West Springfield, Mass.
Miss Ida M. Wing, New Bedford, Mass.
Mrs. L. J. Sanderson, Winchester, Mass.
Mr. B. Treadwell, Grand Lake Stream, Maine.

# ACKNOWLEDGMENTS

Mr. John Lenni Sheldon, Delaware Co., Pa.
Mr. William Fochr, Philadelphia, Pa.
Mrs. W. J. Thomas, Fairhaven, Vt.
Mrs. Lucy G. Haselton, Hampton, N.H.
Miss S. H. Parker, Lancaster, Mass.
Mr. John F. Wilson, Rutland, Vt.
Mr. George Newhall, Swampscott, Mass.
Miss Elizabeth P. Evans, Salem, Mass.
Mr. Frederick L. Avery, Ayer, Mass.
Mr. A. J. Wilcox, Fall River, Mass.
Mr. Thomas E. Mack, New Bedford, Mass.
Mrs. Grace E. Smith, Springfield, Mass.
Mrs. L. M. Hill, Warren, Mass.
Mrs. E. T. Stephens, Springfield, Mass.
Miss Carrie A. Galloupe, Springfield, Mass.
Mrs. T. C. Parsons, Agawam, Mass.
Mrs. Eliza M. Colburn, New Boston, N.H.
Mr. B. F. Spalding, Springfield, Ohio.
Mrs. A. H. Bigelow, Harvard, Mass.
Mrs. Caroline F. Austen, New Bedford, Mass.
Miss Catherine White Grant, Leicester, Mass.
Miss Lydia Porter Warner, Boylston, Mass.
Miss Mary Gerrish Higley, Castleton, Vt.
Miss Honora Harrison, Castleton, Vt.
Miss Sarah N. Harrison, Castleton, Vt.
Mrs. E. R. Parmelee, Brandon, Vt.
Mr. F. E. Gilson, Groton, Mass.
Mrs. J. G. Bradley, Harrisburg, Pa.
Mrs. Alice E. Sargent, Fitchburg, Mass.
Mrs. Lydia D. Waitt, Saugus, Mass.
Messrs. A. Ilsley & Co., Lowell, Mass.
Mrs. Carrie Sprague Sawyer, Dunstable, Mass.
Mr. William W. Brown, Erving, Mass.
Mrs. Paul Ruggles, Carmel, Maine.
Miss Katherine L. Lawrence, Still River, Mass.
Mrs. Mabel P. Robbins, West Acton, Mass.
Miss Kate C. Hennigan, Belmont School, Malden, Mass.
Mrs. Elizabeth Day Totten, Reading, Mass.
Mrs. J. L. Keyes, Still River, Mass.
Capt. C. F. Winch, Georgetown, Mass.
Mrs. Harriet E. Sawyer, Clinton, Mass.
Mr. William H. Graham, South Lancaster, Mass.
Mr. L. Clark, Wilmington, Pa.
Mr. Leonard G. Pells, Cataumet, Mass.
Miss Lillian V. Wilson, New Bedford, Mass.
Mrs. Hannah W. Huston, New Bedford, Mass.
Mrs. Laura A. Underhill, Marshfield Hills, Mass.
Miss Ethel B. France, New Bedford, Mass.
Mrs. E. M. Flint, West Peabody, Mass.
Mrs. W. N. Shipley, East Lynn, Mass.
Mrs. Emily Huston, New Bedford, Mass.
Mrs. Carrie E. Newton, Bangor, Maine.
Mr. Leon A. Goodale, Worcester, Mass.
Mr. Alden Smith, Holden, Mass.

# ACKNOWLEDGMENTS

Mr. Daniel Kinsley, Worcester, Mass.
Mr. Edwin D. Thompson, West Brookfield, Mass.
Mr. William Clough, Lowell, Mass.
Miss Bertha Simpson, Lowell, Mass.
Mrs. E. M. Bowen, Lowell, Mass.
Miss Catherine A. Severy, Chelmsford Centre, Mass.
Miss Adelaide Baker, Lowell, Mass.
Miss Marietta R. Jefferson, Lowell, Mass.
Mr. J. S. Bragdon, Westbrook, Maine.
Mrs. M. C. Owen, West Buxton, Maine.
Mr. Frederic J. Laughlin, Portland, Maine.
Mr. Augustus S. Thayer, Portland, Maine.
Miss Mary Ann Carroll, South-West Harbor, Maine.
Mr. Robert Haines, Island Falls, Maine.
Mrs. Mabel L. Quinn, Levant, Maine.
Miss Lucy Bigelow, Fairfield Centre, Maine.
Mrs. A. H. Walker, Ashland, Maine.
Mrs. George L. Hussey, Dover, Maine.
Mr. A. W. Kelley, Indian River, Maine.
Mrs. S. E. Morrison, Bangor, Maine.
Miss Phylis E. Rapelje, Far Rockaway, N.Y.
Miss Issie Crabbe, Troy, N.Y.
Mr. Dennis E. Wheeler, North Leominster, Mass.
Mr. Francis A. Mason, Caldwell, N.J.
Mrs. H. E. Walton, Eastport, Maine.
Mr. James C. Newland, Vineland, N.J.
Mr. Milton G. Brown, Ocean View, Norfolk, Va.
Mr. A. S. Dalton, Ashland, N.H.
Mrs. Grace M. Weston, Manchester, N.H.
Mrs. Ellen G. S. Wood, Springfield, Mass.
Mrs. L. G. Maranville, Rutland, Vt.
Mr. Henry Williams, Fair Haven, Vt.
Mr. John Hamilton Wilson, Chelmsford, Mass.
Miss L. D. Sanderson, Winchester, Mass.
Mrs. Annie Gohl, Germantown, Philadelphia, Pa.
Mrs. S. A. Noble, Rutland, Vt.
Mrs. Henry C. Mallory, Sudbury, Vt.
Mrs. Frederick A. Hastings, Lancaster Junior College, Lancaster, Mass.
Mrs. Emma Upham Alney, East Brookfield, Mass.
Mrs. Philip H. Loughlin, Westminster, Mass.
Miss Mabel Lillian Warren, Worcester, Mass.
Mr. Henry A. Goodrich, Fitchburg, Mass.
Miss Angela Boutelle, Townsend, Mass.
Mr. H. R. Lloyd, Springfield Republican, Springfield, Mass.
Mrs. Annie Page, Boxboro, Mass.
Mr. William J. Hathaway, New Bedford, Mass.
Miss Angelina Dalton, Salem, Mass.
Miss Mary B. Nichols, South Lancaster, Mass.
Mrs. Daniel N. Wight, West Berlin, Mass.
Miss Anna R. Kittredge, Leominster, Mass.
Miss Emily Brigham, Groton Inn, Groton, Mass.
Mr. Edward C. Gettigan, Philadelphia, Pa.
Mr. Thomas Craighton, Philadelphia, Pa.
Mr. William H. Kettler, Camden Free Public Library, Camden, N.J.

# ACKNOWLEDGMENTS

Mr. L. C. Simon, Philadelphia, Pa.
Mr. Frank Stevens, Stow, Mass.
Mr. and Mrs. Jerome Dwennell, Stow, Mass.
Mr. Eliphelet Tenney, Stow, Mass.
Miss Sarah Houghton, Bolton, Mass.
Leominster Public Library.
Miss Clara Hutchens, Groton, Mass.
Mrs. William C. Endicott, Boston, Mass.
Mr. G. Augustus Peabody, Danvers, Mass.
Mr. Chauncey M. Depew, New York City, N.Y.

# CONTENTS

# CONTENTS

# ILLUSTRATIONS

The illustrations from prints and woodcuts
are taken chiefly from contemporary sources

# INTRODUCTION

METEOROLOGISTS record atmospheric perturbations as scientific facts, as well as electric disturbances, cold waves, heat waves, magnetic currents, and other invisible forces influencing man's physical nature. There are also scientists who are discovering and interpreting the mysteries of sound waves, light waves, radio waves, and their direct influence upon his well-being.

Will they discover some day that far back of all these marvellous phenomena sweeps a force of infinitely rarer, more tenuous, more rapid vibrations that under certain conditions directly affects the mental and spiritual sides of man's nature — stirring them into extreme and even supernormal as well as abnormal activity?

It would account for those strange periods in history when geniuses, poets, reformers, orators, idealists, revivalists, as well as those the world calls "cranks," spring up suddenly on every side — each one responding according to individual capacity and degree of development, as though under the spell of a compelling agitation.

At such times some reach great heights of thought — some are moved to heroic action; pure and highly sensitive natures repudiate the world and its pleasures and turn their thoughts beyond the veil of flesh into the regions of the Spirit. There are also enthusiasts who venture from the beaten track of thought and get bewildered in labyrinths of their own making. There are seemingly sensible people who suddenly accept preposterous theories and become fanatics and run hither and thither propounding vagaries. The voices of orators, preachers, statesmen, can be heard exhorting the emotional masses. There are respectable and well-meaning persons of limited vision who become hysterical — and some of them even go mad.

Just as from the strings of some æolian harps the wind will bring forth harmonies of transcendent beauty, so others lacking resonance will give out only discords. Thus the minds and souls of men and women respond in inverse ratio to undercurrents of mental and spiritual agitation.

Such periods come and go mysteriously. The pages of history are dotted with them. They will return again and yet again as long as human beings inhabit the earth. They are marked by a vital impulse toward breaking away from existing conditions. Restlessness and a sense of change are prevalent — there is a straining upward after ideals that are seemingly unattainable; the public at large is unaccountably stirred and shaken — something unseen and intangible possesses it.

Now in 1843 and 1844, within the recollection of some who are still living, the crest of just such a wave as this was reached. It was a time when the invisible currents found vent through innumerable types of personalities. The reverberation caused by the inspiring public utterances from lips of men now famous rang through the length and breadth of the land. Daniel Webster, Wendell Philips, Garrison, Emerson, and our poets Whittier and Longfellow, and others of that notable group were giving out powerful flashes of light as though suddenly illumined from within. Transcendental-

ism was rampant. New sects were springing up like weeds
in every direction. There was unrest in the churches. The
Unitarians had already come out from the Congregational
Church; now the Universalists were coming out from the
Baptist denomination; these were called "Come-Outers";
and this was causing much excitement and discussion. Theodore Parker had broken away from the Unitarian faith and
was filling Tremont Temple in Boston to overflowing —
hundreds of persons being unable to gain admittance to hear
him lecture on his radical views upon religion. In the midst
of this confusion of ideas a voice was heard coming from the
rural districts — faint and indistinct at first, but continually
increasing in volume as it gave out its strident warning: "Behold, the end of all things is at hand!" The credulous masses
paused and listened with blanched faces.

"Who is saying that?" they asked askance. "A man
named William Miller," some one answers — "'Prophet'
Miller they call him; he's going from village to village and
from town to town and thousands are flocking to hear him."

"Who is he?"

"Why, he's a farmer — born up in Pittsfield, Massachusetts. It seems he lived for some years in Poultney, Vermont, but now his home is in Low Hampton in New York
State; — an earnest good man they say, and seems to know
what he is talking about. He says the Day of Judgment is at
hand and the earth is going to burn up like a scroll, and all
the wicked that are on it. He's warning people to wake up
and look out for what is coming."

Some shrug their shoulders and laugh derisively; others
look serious — but some go home nervous and troubled.

It did not take long for the prophecy to spread; — it seemed to fit in with the times. From one country village to another the word leapt like a tongue of fire until it reached the cities, and then it could not be ignored. Hundreds, and in some places thousands, of people fell under the spell of it; not only the ignorant, but men and women with good minds and erstwhile sound judgment ran breathlessly to and fro — some in terror, others rejoicing, watching for the heavens to open and for the appearance of the Saviour in clouds of glory. The clergy of all denominations were forced to preach vehement sermons, to write and distribute pamphlets, to address meetings, in an attempt to stem the tide of the fanatical tendencies that were only too evidently ready to spring forth and spread far and near as William Miller's intricate calculations and interpretations of the scriptural prophecies were made known, and his method of deciphering the symbols in King Nebuchadnezzar's dream and the prophecies of Daniel and John, including the mysteries of "the ten-horned beast," "the ram and the he-goat," "the little horn," and "the beast rising out of the sea, having seven heads," and "the exceeding Great Horn!"

Edward Everett Hale says, in his biography of James Freeman Clarke: "Meanwhile the idolatry of the letter of Scripture bore legitimate fruit in the proclamation of William Miller that the world would end in the year 1843, on or about the 20th of March. The mathematical instincts of New England especially approved of the additions and subtractions of figures which were found in the Book of Daniel and the Revelation, which, beginning with the dates in Rollin's History, came out neatly by the older calendar at the beginning of 1843."

HARRIET LIVERMORE

# INTRODUCTION xxi

The Reverend Abel C. Thomas, in his "Autobiography" (published in 1852), says: "It required analysis and confutation of every branch of the notion, including both its principles and details of chronology, to stay the progress of the delusion. Despite even multiform demonstrations of its falsity, there were multitudes who clung to it until the last subterfuge of modification was exploded by time."

It must not be supposed, however, that William Miller and his followers were the only ones under the influence of an undue agitation; — 1843 was also a year of great revival among the Shakers. Elders and Eldresses, Brethren and Sisters, were all discovering mediumistic powers within themselves, and were continually conversing with those long dead, and with prophets, martyrs and scriptural characters, even in public meeting — the accompanying exaltation resulting frequently in extreme demonstrations of hysteria. Emerson, who wrote an article in the "Dial" in July of that same year on the "Convention of Friends of Universal Reform," says of that gathering: "If the assembly was disorderly, it was picturesque. Madmen, Madwomen, Men with beards, Dunkers, Muggletonians, Come-Outers, Groaners, Agrarians, Seventh-Day Baptists, Quakers, Abolitionists, Calvinists, Unitarians, and Philosophers — all came successively to the top."

It is rather impressive to note the comment of Margaret Fuller Ossoli upon this occasion: "Amid all these wild gospellers," she writes, "came and went the calm figure of Emerson, peaceful and undisturbed." [1]

[1] Thomas Wentworth Higginson, *Life of Margaret Fuller Ossoli.*

Again, referring to this period, Octavius Brooks Frothingham speaks of it in his biography of Theodore Parker as "a remarkable agitation of mind," and adds that "it did not seem to be communicated — to spread by contagion; but it was rather an intellectual experience produced by some latent causes in the air. No special class of people were affected by it. While in Boston the little knot of transcendentalists — Channing, Ripley, Margaret Fuller, Emerson, Alcott, Hedge, Parker — were discussing the problems of philosophy at the Tremont House and elsewhere, the farmers of the country and the plain folks of Cape Cod were as full of the new spirit as they."

It was the farmers of the country who were the first to respond to William Miller's cry of warning, but it soon spread into the industrial centres and among tradespeople, until finally some of every class were numbered among his followers.

But it must not be supposed that the part of his prophecy that dealt with the Second Coming of our Lord in clouds of glory belonged exclusively to William Miller at this time. A converted Jew in Palestine, named Joseph Wolff, who was well known in England, was predicting the Advent would be 1847; but his theory regarding it differed wholly from that of our New England prophet, inasmuch as he claimed that the Saviour would appear from the Mount of Olives — enter Jerusalem, and there reign for a thousand years over the twelve tribes of Israel. Then there was also the beautiful but eccentric Harriet Livermore,[1] daughter of a member of Con-

---

[1] Harriet Livermore's father, Judge St. Low Livermore, was originally from New Hampshire, but he moved to Lowell early in his married life and lived

gress from Massachusetts, and one of the characters represented in Whittier's poem "Snow-Bound," who had been preaching the near approach of the Second Coming for several years, in many different parts of the country, as well as on four different occasions in the Hall of Representatives at Washington where great crowds gathered to hear her. Her views coincided with those of Joseph Wolff, only she went a step farther and claimed to have convincing proof that the American Indians were descendants of the lost tribe of Israel, and urged transporting them to Palestine so that they might take their rightful place in the Millennial Kingdom.

There was also Lady Hester Stanhope, a niece of William Pitt, and a granddaughter of the great Lord Chatham, who had installed herself in a home on Mount Lebanon in order to be ready for "the Coming." In "Snow-Bound" she is referred to as "The Crazy Queen of Lebanon," and no wonder, for the poor lady was so deluded that she actually kept two rare and beautiful white Arab horses in her stable ready and waiting for the great event. On one of these she planned that our Lord would enter Jerusalem and she intended to follow Him on the other!

Whittier positively asserts, in a letter written to the Rev-

there until he was sent to Congress. His first wife's name was Mehitable Harms, and after her death he married Sarah Crease Stackpole, of Boston, who was Harriet's mother. He died in 1832 and was buried in the Granary Burying-Ground in Boston. The tomb is No. 77, adjacent to Tremont Street, and has a costly bronze coat of arms set in the wall separating the wall from the street. He had three nephews who were prominent in their times: the Right Reverend Charles Grafton, Bishop of Fond du Lac; Father Edward Welch, a great preacher in his day at the Church of the Immaculate Conception in Boston; and Mr. Guerney Grafton, an art connoisseur who lived in Paris. Judge St. Low Livermore had two daughters, Harriet and Caroline; the latter married Josiah Abbott, of Lowell, who moved to Boston and was well known as a prominent lawyer.

erend Abel C. Thomas on September 18, 1879, that Harriet
Livermore told him of a visit she made to Lady Hester Stanhope while she was on one of her pilgrimages to the Holy
Land, and he adds that these two quarrelled on account of
the former claiming the right to be the one to ride the spare
horse when the Great Day should come, instead of the owner.
The Reverend C. V. A. Van Dyke, who had frequently met
Harriet Livermore in Syria, doubts, however, the fact of the
two women having met, but in a letter written to the Reverend S. T. Livermore he says: "Had there been a meeting I
would have given my little finger to have witnessed it — it
would have been diamond cut diamond; — the haughty aris-
tocratic English woman, and the fearless republican. I doubt
not there would have been some sharp passages between
them." [1]

(N.B. — Poor deluded things! may they be forgiven!)

This bears out an assertion made by Margaret Fuller Ossoli, that "One very marked trait of the period was that the
agitation reached all circles." [2]

Now William Miller's views differed widely from those of
these three self-made prophets. He not only predicted the
date of the Second Coming of our Saviour, but he also predicted the destruction by fire of the earth and the wicked
that were upon it. To sum it up, his belief was as follows:
"That Christ would appear a second time in the clouds of
heaven some time between 1843 and 1844; that He would
then raise the righteous dead and judge them together with
the righteous living, who would be caught up to meet Him in

[1] Rev. S. T. Livermore, *Harriet Livermore — The Pilgrim Stranger.*
[2] Thomas Wentworth Higginson, *Life of Margaret Fuller Ossoli.*

LADY HESTER STANHOPE IN HER VILLA ON MT. LEBANON

the air; that He would purify the earth by fire causing the
wicked and all their works to be consumed in the general conflagration, and would shut up their souls in the place prepared for the Devil and his angels; that the saints would live
and reign with Christ on the new earth a thousand years;
that then Satan and the wicked dead would be raised, this
being the second resurrection, and, being judged, would
make war upon the saints, be defeated and cast down to hell
forever"; or, as the Reverend John Henry Hopkins, D.D.,
describes it, in a pamphlet published in 1843 refuting Miller's
theory: "and consign them together to the Lake of Fire,
and the smoke of their torment shall ascend forever and
ever."

Such were the conditions in 1843 and 1844, when the
strange religious agitation swept thousands away from the
path of normal reasoning right here and throughout the Eastern States only one generation ago! To many it seemed like
a sort of religious farce; to others it was comedy — pure and
simple; some were grievously shocked and troubled; many
jeered; but to the misguided and deluded ones most closely
involved the end was tragedy — overwhelming disappointment and tragedy.

Just as delirium rages before a fever breaks, leaving the patient limp and scarcely breathing, so the pitiful, simple, credulous souls who followed William Miller up to the Great Day
of his prophetic calculations were left prostrated and dazed
by their shattered hopes.

The years 1843–1844 — years of exaltation — of transcendent visions — of beatific aspirations — of idealistic impossible experiments — of high and balanced thoughts and

strange unbalanced ones; at the end of which the dreamers awoke and the velocity of the mysterious invisible currents slowed down and gradually subsided.

As for William Miller, despite all that his detractors have said of him, he was a truly earnest and devout man, but self-hypnotized into believing in his own method of calculation and his own presumptuous powers of interpretation. He failed as all must fail who venture to attempt to crowd into a space of finite days and years the sum of infinite incalculable mysteries. The pathos, the assumption, the foolishness, the ignorance of poor blind human nature, with its pitiful inconsequence and its inconsistencies! — the humor of it, and here and there the beauty of it will be found in the following meagre scraps that remain to tell the tale of this extraordinary episode in our religious history.

# DAYS OF DELUSION

# DAYS OF DELUSION

∴

## CHAPTER I

### EARLY YEARS

"A youth to whom was given
So much of earth, so much of heaven."

"WHAT kind of a man could William Miller have been?" is the wondering question often asked when the Millerite excitement of 1843 is spoken of.

Well — he was what one might call a *character*. If he had been told in his youth that some day he would be prophesying the near approach of the Day of Judgment and the destruction of the world by fire, he would have been as surprised as anybody. The paths of Destiny sometimes lead into unexpected pastures.

To begin with, in his childhood William Miller was the kind of a boy who would creep downstairs with as little noise as possible after his parents and all his brothers and sisters had gone to bed and thrust some pitch-wood into the embers smouldering in the depths of the broad brick chimney in the kitchen so as to get light from the flames, and then stretch himself at full length upon the hearth and read with trembling ecstasy of the thrilling adventures of Robinson Crusoe and Robert Boyle, and all those heroes of fiction so dear to the heart of every normal lad who conceals within him a touch of romance, of poetry, and chivalry.

Then, too, the difficulty of procuring the precious volumes enhanced their value to him. It was only when he could earn money chopping wood "out of school hours" that he could ever buy one, and each book added to his meager store was loved as a friend. He was the oldest of sixteen children and the only one of them that cared for books. His parents, who were quiet, respectable people in humble circum- stances — good Baptists both of them and firm adherents of that faith — were troubled by the desire he showed to read whatever he could lay his hands on. The father was just a typical farmer such as can be found anywhere in our country districts — a God-fearing, industrious man, able to feed and clothe his family upon the resources of his farm, but unable to give them more than country villages provide in the way of education.

So William Miller went to the district school as all the country children did, but he was better than any of his com- rades at his lessons, and after a while it became a matter of comment that he was likely to outstrip his teacher in knowl- edge if he persisted in reading outside of school hours, and it was not approved of by some. But there happened to be several well-to-do men in the neighborhood who looked upon it differently, and they became enough interested in him to lend him books that were far beyond his means to buy, and these he pored over with a joy that was incomprehensible to his parents, who looked upon this desire for literature on the part of their eldest son with a good deal of disapproval and suspicion as well as apprehension. But this did not deter him; in spite of their admonitions he still kept on, and as he grew older a longing for a real education beset him with such intensity that, as he afterwards expressed it, "it seemed almost essential to his existence"; but it was not to be — work in the fields and helping out on the farm claimed all his spare hours. So he had to get what learning he could through his own efforts — reading all that he could find within his reach with so much perseverance and tenacity that when he had acquired the age of manhood he had left his associates far behind him in matters of book lore and was accorded a degree of consideration by his fellow townspeople that was unusual in one so young. By this time his parents had changed their views in regard to him. They deplored the fact that they could not help him to get the knowledge that he longed for. The best they could do was to let him have more time for his reading and they gave him a room to himself — a luxury unlooked for in so large a family — and there he absorbed a heterogeneous mixture of history, poetry, fiction, etc., with no instructor or guide to point the way other than his own inclination.

For the young people of the place "he became a sort of scribbler general," and his biographer tells us, "If any one wanted verses made, or a letter to send, or some ornamental or symbolic design to be interpreted by the tender passion, or anything which required extra task or fancy in the use of the pen, it was pretty sure to be planned if not executed by him." [1]

He was married a few months after his twenty-first birthday to Miss Lucy Smith, of Poultney, Vermont. The wedding took place on June 30, 1803, and there they started life together on a small farm.

[1] Sylvester Bliss, *Life of William Miller.*

It so happened that there was quite a sizable library in the village which especially attracted young Miller, and whatever time he could spare from his farm work was given to poring over the books he found there. It must be said that he was extremely fortunate in his choice of a wife. Instead of trying to draw him away from the bookshelves, the young woman encouraged him to indulge his craving for knowledge, realizing that his spare time was limited. It was not long before some of the superior men of the place — those with bigger farms and broader outlook — began to notice him and to watch him with some interest. It was unusual to find a young man newly wedded poring over the old musty volumes in the village library instead of keeping out in the sunshine with his bride during his spare hours, and their curiosity was stirred.

It was just about a year or two after the young couple had started farming in Poultney that exceptional preparations were being made in the village to celebrate the Fourth of July, and every one was entering into the spirit of it with great enthusiasm, including, of course, young Miller and his wife, and while the former was hoeing in his cornfield he felt inspired to write a patriotic hymn for the occasion. That evening, after he had finished his farm work and attended to the chores, he sat down and wrote verses that could be sung to the tune of "Delight" — an old song familiar to every one in those days.

Now the appointed marshal for the day was Squire Ashley, a near neighbor of his, and, being somewhat diffident in regard to his poetical effusion, the young man took some time to consider how he could bring it to this gentleman's attention without appearing presumptuous. He thought it over during the night, and the next morning he walked over to Squire Ashley's farm, and, catching a glimpse of Mrs. Ashley sitting sewing close to the sitting-room window, he managed to slip his manuscript on to the window sill without attracting attention and hurried away.

When the good lady looked up from her sewing, her eyes fell upon it, and, thinking it was something belonging to her husband, she took it to him and he opened it and read what was written inside.

"Why, what's this? — what's this poem?" he asked his wife.

"I thought it was something belonging to you," she replied, opening her eyes wide with surprise — "I found it on the window sill."

"Well — that's certainly strange! — why, but these are fine words that express fine sentiments! — and the footnote states it can be sung to the tune of 'Delight' — We'll sing it at the celebration — it's just what we need!"

The Squire immediately sought out several friends and deputed them to make numerous copies which could be distributed among the village people and thus enable all present to join in the singing. There was great curiosity expressed as to who the mysterious author could be and it created quite a stir.

When the hour came for the celebration and the people had assembled, they were told to form in line and apply in turn for one of the copies so as to sing this newly acquired patriotic hymn with a good big volume of sound. Mr. Kenricks, the Baptist minister, stood where he could watch the face of each person as he came forward to receive a copy, and, seeing young William Miller's countenance flushed with embarrassment as he put his hand out, he became convinced that he was the one they all were looking for. Consequently, he questioned him closely and drew forth an admission from him regarding the authorship of the hymn which they were preparing to sing, whereupon all lifted up their voices and sang it with enthusiasm. It was declared to be a great success, and perfectly suited to the occasion.

The verses are as follows:

> "Our Independence dear,
>   Bought with the price of blood,
>   Let us receive with care,
>   And trust our Maker God,
>       For He's the tower
>       To which we fly;
>       His grace is nigh
>       In every hour.
>
> "Nor shall Columbia's sons
>   Forget the price it cost,
>   As long as water runs,
>   Or leaves are nipped by frost.
>       Freedom is thine;
>       Let millions rise,
>       Defend the prize
>       Through rolling time!
>
> "There was a Washington,
>   A man of noble fame,
>   Who led Columbia's sons
>   To battle on the plain;
>   With skill they fought;
>   The British host
>   With all their boast
>   Soon came to naught!
>
> "Let traitors hide their heads
>   And party quarrels cease;

Our foes are struck with dread,
When we declare for peace.
   Firm let us be,
   And rally round
   The glorious sound
   Of liberty!"

"This production with other prose and poetry," so says his biographer, "made him at once notable in the community and secured for him a wide circle of friends. The young folks made his house a place of common resort to which they gathered to spend their leisure hours, while he and his wife became the central unit which drew them together and kept all in motion." Things were looking bright for them; the farm was prospering, and young William Miller had become a member of the Masonic fraternity in which "he advanced to the highest degree which the lodges then in the country, or in that region could confer." [1] More than that, he was soon appointed to the position of Constable, and in 1809 to the office of Sheriff, and he was well on the road to the promotion of High Sheriff when, to the amazement of his friends, he became bitten with an overwhelming desire to enter the Army.

"What strong impulse could have turned him off in that direction?" asks his biographer; "already the business of his office had placed him in easy circumstances. Such was the amount of his business that he kept two horses, one of which he drove, while the other was kept up to rest week by week, alternately. He enjoyed the respect and unbounded confidence of the public. His preference for the Army, so far as we know, sprang from two motives: first, he desired to partici-

[1] Sylvester Bliss, *Life of William Miller.*

pate in the glory which rested on the memory of those he
held most dear in the history of his country and his family
(his father had fought in the Revolution); secondly, he
hoped to enjoy a more inviting exhibition of human nature
in the scenes of military life than experience or books had
afforded in civil life. He was satisfied with the trial of what
was around him and wished to try a new field." This is
stated by himself in his published "Memoirs." "In the
mean time I continued my studies," he writes, "storing my
mind with historical knowledge. The more I read, the more
dreadfully corrupt did the character of man appear. I could
discern no bright spot in the history of the past. Those con-
querors of the world and heroes of history were apparently
but demons in human form. All the sorrow, suffering, and
misery in the world seemed to be increased in proportion to
the power they attained over their fellows. I began to feel
very distrustful of all men. In this state of mind I entered
the service of my country. I fondly cherished the idea that I
should find one bright spot at least in the human character as
a star of hope; — a *love of country — Patriotism.*"

This tone of pessimism and depression which was beginning to tarnish the brightness of his outlook was due to two
things, the influence of the men with whom he had daily intercourse, and the books that he had been reading. A course
of study of the works of Voltaire, Hume, Volney, Paine,
Ethan Allen, and others in the same line of thought, had
borne fruit after their kind. Now these friends of his were
respectable, moral men, and good citizens as well, but they
did not trouble themselves about spiritual matters, they
cared only for the material world, and most of them were

avowed deists — men who in an offhand way admitted the existence of a Creator, but repudiated all belief in the revealed religion of our Saviour — and in their ignorance they ridiculed and made fun of William Miller's strict ways and religious belief, and twitted him for going to church. The Millers were all Baptists, by nature devout, and looked upon religion with reverence; but this perpetual scoffing on the part of his friends proved to be more than William could stand and he turned about and declared openly that he had become a deist. His biographer describes the deplorable effect of this change upon his character:

"During this period the effect of deism upon him was such as to make him treat the Bible and all sacred subjects with pitiable levity. He seemed to take a sort of defiant pleasure in banishing from his memory the impressions of his early life, and he gave to his sceptical associates an assurance that he had mastered his *superstition*, as they deemed it, by performing for their sport the devotions of the worship to which he had been accustomed, and especially by mimicking the devotional peculiarities of some of his own family relations. One of these was his grandfather Phelps, pastor of the Baptist Church at Orwell; the other was his uncle, Elihu Miller, who was settled as pastor of the Baptist Church at Low Hampton. These honorable ambassadors of Christ, and other pious relatives, often visited Mr. Miller's house at Poultney, and although he received them with affection and respect, and entertained them in the most generous manner, he was in the habit of imitating with the most ludicrous gravity their words, tones of voice, gestures, fervency, and even the grief they might manifest for such as himself, to afford a kind of entertainment for his sceptical associates, which they seemed to enjoy with peculiar relish."

"Little did he think," his biographer pertinently remarks, "that he was measuring to these faithful men what was to be measured to him again — pressed down, shaken together, and running over!"

His wife and parents were almost prostrated with grief at the revelation of this phase of his character, as opposed to all that he had been before, and which was so alien to their simple and serious faith.

"There was more than one heart that was almost inconsolably afflicted by this conduct of Mr. Miller," his biographer continues. "His mother knew of it, and it was as the bitterness of death to her. Some of his pious sisters witnessed with tears his improprieties, and when his mother spoke of the affliction to her father Phelps, he would console her by saying; 'Don't afflict yourself too deeply about William. There is something for him to do yet in the cause of God.'"

Such was the state of his mind when he entered the Army as a Lieutenant. His commission is dated July 21, 1810, and is signed by Jonas Galusha, Governor of Vermont. A copy of his oath written on the back of his commission is as follows:

"I, William Miller, solemnly swear that I will be true and faithful to the State of Vermont; that I will not directly or indirectly do any act or thing injurious to the Constitution or Government thereof as established by Convention. So help me God. I also swear that I will support the Constitution of the United States.

"WILLIAM MILLER

"*August* 13, 1811."

"The foregoing oaths were taken and subscribed to before me,

"CALEB HANDY, JR., Brig. Gen."

All this happened a year before the declaration of war between the United States and England.

"On the 18th of June, 1812, the declaration was made in due form; and the first note of preparation found Mr. Miller with hundreds of his hardy and patriotic Green Mountain neighbors ready to take the field. A very short time after, it was announced that he would take his place at the head of a company of State Volunteers. On the day after the date of the act of the State Government of Vermont, which authorized the raising of such a body, his captain's commission is dated." [1]

It was expected that the fighting would take place in the direction of Burlington, and Captain Miller's company was ordered there, as well as all the other volunteers who came from that part of the country. An accident happened to him while on the march to Burlington which not only came near being fatal to him, but which left its mark upon him, and it is a question whether it did not make deeper inroads upon his health than were recognized at the time. He described his unfortunate experience to his wife in the following letter:

"CAMP AT BURLINGTON
"*June 13th,* 1813
"DEAR LUCY:

"I am now at this place after a fatiguing march. My feet are all worn out, and my body is very sore. On our march

[1] Sylvester Bliss, *Life of William Miller.*

from Bennington to this place I met with an accident which almost deprived me of life. The last day of our march, my feet and ankles being very lame, I hired a passage in a wagon with four or five of my brother officers. Capt. Clark and myself got into the hind part of the wagon, and while fixing the seat the horses started and threw me out. I fell on the back of my head, and they have since informed me that I lay as if dead for fifteen or twenty minutes. They put me into the wagon and carried me five or six miles before I came to my senses.

"I have not much of consequence to write. We expect the British in at Burlington every hour. There were about a thousand men came in yesterday from Bennington and Windsor, and we are ready to meet them with any force they can bring against us. I have nothing more to write but to subscribe myself          "Your ever loving husband
                              "WILLIAM MILLER."

On the very day that he wrote this letter he received notice that he had been transferred from the Volunteers of the State of Vermont to the rank of Lieutenant in the Regular Army of the United States, as the following order will show:

                    "ENCAMPMENT BURLINGTON
                         "*June* 13, 1813
"SIR:
    "You are hereby commanded to repair to the County of Rutland, and there attend to the Recruiting Service for the 30th Regt. Infantry in the U.S. Army. You will govern yourself by the laws of the United States, and return to this post when commanded.
                    [Signed] "MASON ORMSBIE, Maj. Inf'ry
"To Lieut. Miller, U.S. Army."

ELDER SYLVESTER BLISS

In remarking upon this change his biographer says: "Such a transfer is considered honorable in the military sense; and the change of service, which allowed him to enjoy the comforts of home and the attention of friends while suffering from his late accident, must have been very acceptable." [1]

But he had not been there a month when he received an imperative command from Headquarters as follows:

"CANTONMENT BURLINGTON
"*July 7th*, 1813
"LIEUT. W. MILLER, at Poultney,

"You are hereby commanded to join your regiment at Burlington immediately, and report yourself to the Commanding Officer.

"ELIAS FASSET, Col. 30th Infantry."

Again came the hurried good-byes and the departure, and fortunately he little suspected what awaited him at Burlington. Shortly after joining his regiment the dreaded army fever broke loose and spread rapidly among the troops, and the fatalities were so numerous that orders were issued to remove the bulk of the army to higher land. But Lieutenant Miller, who succumbed to the fever quickly, owing to his health being weakened on account of his accident, was too ill to be removed, and he and a few other severe cases remained to fight their way back to health where they were.

When autumn came he had practically recovered with the exception of a terrible sore upon his arm. As he suffered very much from it, an operation was advised. The following anecdote regarding it reveals a very human quality in his

[1] Sylvester Bliss, *Life of William Miller*.

character which is worth noting and which his biographer
relates: "He was somewhat displeased by the rudeness of
the thoughtless medical students or surgeons' mates, who
too often seemed to think that a disabled soldier is good for
nothing but to cut up for experiments. As they handled the
diseased limb one day somewhat roughly, and spoke very
lightly of its amputation as a matter of course, he reminded
them that his sword arm was still sound; and putting his
hand on the hilt of his sword before him, gave them to
understand that whatever might be advised in the case, he
should not submit to any unnecessary pain for their amusement. They understood him and it ended their rudeness.
He managed to keep his arm, and was able to join his regiment which was now in active service, searching for the
enemy on the Canadian frontier."

The year 1814 came at last, which was to be the crucial
period of the war. In August of that year Lieutenant Miller
was promoted to the rank of Captain in the Regular Army.
He received the following summons that same month:

"BURLINGTON, *August* 12, 1814

"To WM. MILLER, Capt. in the 30th In'y.
"SIR:

"You are ordered to report yourself to the Commanding
Officer of said regiment without delay at Plattsburg.

"I am, Sir, with respect, etc., etc.

"ELIAS FASSET

"Col. 30th and Comd. recruiting."

It was close upon the heels of his arrival at camp that the
thrilling moment came for which our army had been waiting,

and an extract from the following letter to his wife, dated September 4, 1814, reveals the suppressed excitement under which Captain Miller was laboring:

"The British," he writes, "are within ten miles of this place and we expect a battle to-morrow; and I think they must be d——d fools if they do not attack us, as they are ten or eleven thousand strong, and we are only fifteen hundred, but every man is determined to do his duty. It may be my lot to fall; — if I do I will fall bravely. Remember, you will never hear from me if I am a coward.

"I must close, as it is almost eleven o'clock.

"Remember your

"WILLIAM MILLER."

How vividly these few lines reveal the suspense and excitement that were beating in every one of those fifteen hundred courageous hearts!

They had to wait a week, but at last the looked-for moment came on the 11th of September.

It was a beautiful mild morning and our warships rode quietly at anchor, while all about them sparkled the blue waters of Plattsburg Bay in the early autumn sunshine. Suddenly the lookout boat gave a sharp warning of the approach of the enemy, and presently the British fleet could be seen passing Cumberland Head, while at the same moment the firing of the royal salute shook the air and echoed from shore to shore.

Immediately every sailor on our ships and every soldier in the forts bordering on the lake sprang to their posts. — The battle had begun.

History has eloquently recorded Commodore Macdon-
ough's victory and described the precipitous retreat of the
British land forces, commanded by Sir George Provost, with
a loss of twenty-five hundred men in killed, wounded, and
missing after the naval defeat.

The following jubilant letters written by Captain Miller
paint a vivid picture of that memorable day. The first was
written to Judge Stanley, of Poultney, and reads as follows:

"FORT SCOTT, *Sept.* 11, 1814
"20 minutes past two o'clock P.M.

"SIR:

" *It is over! It is done!* The British fleet has struck to the
American flag! Great slaughter on both sides! They are in
plain view where I am now writing. My God! the sight was
majestic, it was noble, it was grand!

"This morning at ten o'clock the British opened a very
heavy and destructive fire upon us, both by water and by
land; then congreve rockets flew like hailstones about us, and
round shot and grape from every quarter. You have no idea
of the battle! Our force was small, but how bravely they
fought! Sir Lord George Provost feels bad. His land force
may expect to meet their fate if our Militia do their duty;
but in time of action they were not to be seen. The action on
water lasted only two hours and ten minutes; the firing from
their batteries has but just ceased — ours is still continuing;
the small arms are now just coming to action. I have no
time to write any more; you must conceive what we feel, for
I cannot describe it. I am satisfied that I can fight; I know
that I am no coward; therefore call on Mr. Loomis to drink
my health, and I will pay the shot. Three of my men are

wounded by a shell which burst within two feet of me. The boat from the fleet, which has just landed under our fort, says the British Commodore is killed.

"Out of three hundred on board their ship twenty-five remain alive. Some of our officers who have been on board say the blood is knee-deep.

"Their force we have taken consists of one ship, thirty-six guns, one brig of eighteen guns, and two sloops.

"*Huzza! Huzza!* Twenty or thirty British prisoners taken by our Militia have just arrived in fort! I can write no more, for the time grows dubious.

"Yours forever

"Wm. Miller.

"Give my compliments to all, and send this to my wife."

A horse and rider galloping through the village of Poultney shouted the news of the victory, and William Miller's wife, waiting with an anxious heart, was one of the first to hear his coming. It seemed not the space of a moment when the bells pealed forth; the people shouted and sang for joy, and the greatest excitement prevailed.

Captain Miller's letter to his wife gives a graphic account of that memorable September 11th which is worth reading. It not only describes the battle, but between the lines one gets glimpses that reveal something of the character of the man:

"Fort Scott, *Sept.* 12, 1811

"7 o'clock, morning

"Dear Wife:

"Yesterday was a day of great joy. *We have conquered! We have drove them!* About nine o'clock A.M. yesterday the

British fleet fired a salute as they passed Cumberland Head; it was a token for a general engagement. About twenty minutes after they hove in sight. How majestic! How noble! Our fleet lay in Plattsburg Bay; and like a saucy Yankee paid no attention to their royal salute! The British fleet still bearing down upon us, bold as a lion — in a moment we were all prepared for action. The British had thrown up a number of batteries on all sides of us. The next minute the cannon began playing — spitting their fires in every quarter. What a scene! All was dreadful! — nothing but roaring and groaning for about six or eight hours. I cannot describe to you our situation. The fort I was in was exposed to every shot. Bombs, rockets, and shrapnel shells fell thick as hailstones. Three of my men were wounded, and one killed, but none that were from Poultney or that quarter.

"In one hour and forty-five minutes the enemy's fleet was conquered. My God! what a slaughter on all sides! — out of three hundred on board of one ship, twenty-four alone remained unhurt! I cannot describe to you the general joy!

"At sundown our forts fired a national salute, accompanied by a tune called 'Yankee Doodle,' and each gun was loaded with an eighteen-pound shot. This soon frightened our foe to that degree that this morning at daybreak not a soul was to be seen; and they went off in so great a hurry that not one article of their baggage could they carry away. Some they burnt, and some they left behind. Their loss in killed and wounded is immense, besides one hundred taken prisoners, and three or four hundred deserters. Our loss was not so great, but considerable. Every officer and soldier is now singing for joy, and there is nothing now heard but the

11th day of September, and Lord George Provost retreating for Canada. You may well conceive by my unconnected mode of writing that I am as joyful as any of them. A naval and land engagement within the compass of a mile or two, and fifteen or twenty thousand engaged at one and the same time, is superior to anything my eyes ever beheld before. How grand! how noble, yet how awful! The roaring of cannon, the bursting of bombs, the whizzing of balls, the popping of small arms, the cracking of timbers, the shrieks of the dying, the groans of the wounded, the commands of the officers, the swearing of soldiers, the smoke, the fire; — everything conspires to make the scene of a battle both awful and grand!

"The fort I was in was on the bank of the lake and in plain view of everything which passed.

"Remember me to all my friends; and in the mean time accept of me as I am

"Faithfully yours

"WM. MILLER."

One of the incidents that gave him the greatest satisfaction as a culmination of that never-to-be forgotten day, and in which he was deputed to take part, was preparing the body of the English Commodore for burial. To quote from his biography: "The honor paid to the dead by the Americans was as worthy of remembrance as the bravery with which they fought." [1]

Thus ended the military career of Captain Miller. He retired from the Army in June, 1815, and sought the little

[1] Sylvester Bliss, *Life of William Miller.*

farm in Poultney once more, where his devoted wife and a little son now awaited him. Once again he systematically planted his crops and in the fullness of time harvested them. Again his neighbors wondered to see him spend his spare hours poring over a large, ponderous volume — not in the library this time, but in the seclusion of his own home. Nor was it Voltaire, nor Hume, nor Volney, nor Paine that absorbed his interest. A change had come over William Miller. Now it was the Book of books; — the Bible, with its magnificent interpretations of Life and Death — its mysterious prophecies, its glorious promises, its inspired diction that held him spellbound.

Who can tell how and why such changes come?

The following chapter will attempt to trace the mental processes that turned the retired soldier into the man known far and wide as "Prophet" Miller, with a newly awakened power to sway mighty gatherings of people, with a gift of vividly pictorial language — with a personality that baffled even those bitterly opposed to his convictions; — chastened in spirit; more or less broken in health; repentant of past scepticism, and calling upon those spiritually asleep to awaken and repent, for the end of the world was at hand!

# CHAPTER II

## THE AWAKENING

"My thoughts on awful subjects roll:
Damnation and the dead."

DR. WATTS

THERE were two incidents that occurred during William Miller's military career, just as he was about to return to civil life, that swept his thoughts into new channels. The first was during a night in camp, and at an hour when he was making his rounds to see that all was quiet and that his men were in their tents. While performing this duty, he espied a light gleaming in one of them and he heard a low voice speaking in tones of great intensity. He stopped short and listened. Presently he heard other voices, also lowered, and he was on the alert in a moment. There had been great difficulty in preventing the men from gambling in camp, and strict rules had been given out against it. For a moment he thought he had caught some transgressors red-handed. Drawing nearer to the tent, he stopped and listened again. There was a pause, and then the voice he had heard at first began to speak again — this time in tones of apparent supplication. He realized now that the man was praying. Shrugging his shoulders impatiently, he strode off. Life in the Army had not lessened his miserable habit of ridiculing all religious observances, and in thinking over what he had heard, he made up his mind to play a joke upon this young soldier the next day, and to give him a good fright regarding the sound of voices that had issued from his tent during the night. Accordingly, when morning came, he summoned him and stood awaiting him with an ugly frown upon his brow.

"Sergeant Willey," he said, addressing the young man as he approached him, "you know that it is contrary to Army regulations to have any gambling in the tents at night. I was sorry to see your tent lit up for that purpose last night. We cannot have any gambling at such times. You must put a stop to it at once. I hope I shall not have to speak to you again about it."

The young soldier, taken completely by surprise, flushed to the roots of his hair. "We were not gambling, Sir," he stammered, lowering his eyes.

There was something in the boyish, candid face before him and in the tones of his voice that touched Captain Miller in spite of himself. He cast the impression away from his mind and went on with his joke. He believed he could enjoy forcing Sergeant Willey to confess what he had been doing and he then planned to ridicule it.

"Yes, you were gambling!" he cried, contradicting him with added severity, "and it won't do! What else could you have your tent lighted up for all the evening if you were not gambling?"

The young soldier drew himself up to his full height, and, squaring his shoulders, looked Captain Miller in the face.

"We were praying, Sir," he answered, very quietly and simply.

There was so much dignity and truth in the answer and the manner of delivering it that Captain Miller suddenly found himself abashed and humiliated. Without another word he turned on his heel and walked away. The brave and earnest eyes that had met his so fearlessly troubled him. He had indulged in gambling himself at times, and he recalled this, and the fact now shamed him as he thought over the joke he had tried to play which had failed so lamentably. He was more disturbed than he cared to admit. He sat up the following night trying to shake off the impression the occurrence had made upon him, but it would not leave him. He pondered over the courage displayed by the group of young soldiers whose voices he had heard in the tent, and their fearless independence in uniting together right in the rough and brutalizing atmosphere of the camp to pray for the safety of their souls. He felt shaken by it, and he thought of his own soul — what was its condition? Had he drugged it into so deep a sleep that it could not awaken? He remembered that sometimes — indeed often — he, like those about him, had made free use of the name of the Almighty. This also troubled him now.

"One day," he states in his "Memoirs," "I detected myself in the act of taking the name of God in vain — a habit I had acquired in the service; and I was instantly convicted of its sinfulness."

Now, in spite of all William Miller's much-vaunted deism, it needed but little probing to discover an ingenuous, simple, kindly nature hidden under the outer coating of his heart. The following statement made by his biographer who was his personal friend will show this:

"All who have any knowledge of the question will confirm that his personal integrity and official honor were such throughout his connection with the Army as to command in an almost unexampled degree the respect and affection of all who were under him as an officer, and the hearty confidence and esteem of his official associates.

"For years after the war closed, it was a common thing for his brethren in arms to turn aside from the great route of travel five or six miles only to enjoy a short interview with one to whom they were strongly attached; and some of the less provident, feeling sure he would receive them with a sort of fatherly sympathy, which a poor unfortunate soldier seldom finds in the world, were accustomed to tarry with him some days or weeks at a time." [1]

The second incident which made a deep impression upon him was when a friend of his named Spencer died of fever in camp. During the latter's illness, Captain Miller had a long talk with him of which he wrote an account to his wife. It is evident that this conversation, followed by the death of his friend, again touched the chord within him that had long been lying dormant. Watching the life forces wane and finally pass out from the body of one who had been a trusted comrade seems to have stirred him to the depths of his being, and to have started questions in his mind regarding the existence of the soul after death that bewildered him and caused poignant distress and apprehension.

"But a short time," he wrote to his wife, "and like Spencer I shall be no more. It is a solemn thought. Yet could I be sure of another life there would be nothing terrific; — but to go out like an extinguished taper is insupportable — the thought is doleful. No! rather let me cling to that hope which warrants a never-ending existence; — a future spring

[1] Sylvester Bliss, *Life of William Miller.*

where troubles shall cease and tears find no conveyance; — where never-ending spring shall flourish, and love, pure as the driven snow, rest in every breast.

"Dear Lucy do write me, and let me know how you pass your time. Good evening — I am troubled.

"WM. MILLER."

It can be seen that his mind was tossed over these questions when he received his discharge from the Army that same year and returned to the humble occupations of a farmer. During his absence of seven or more years, his father, whose home had been for some time in Low Hampton, had died, and in order to be near his mother he left Poultney and moved his family, which now consisted of his wife and a young son, to a farm near hers, comprising about two hundred acres. Here he built one of those typical New England farmhouses, painted white with green blinds, that are so familiar to those who know the country, and began to farm in earnest. But the manual labor did not suffice to quiet his troubled spirit. He was facing now a battle worse than any he had been engaged in during his military career, but it was no bodily conflict this time — it was a mental experience, fraught with distress and anguish of mind; — fears and doubts assailing him on one side, and a yearning for faith and the joy of peace and the security of a quiet conscience on the other. Even his devoted wife could do nothing to help him. She was forced to stand aside and watch his misery in silence and pray for relief to come.

In referring to this unhappy period in his "Memoirs," he says: "I thought to seek for that happiness which had always eluded my pursuit in my former occupations, in the domestic circle. For a little space, a care and burden was taken off my mind; but after a while I felt the need of some more active employment. My life became too monotonous. I had lost all those pleasing prospects which in youth I expected to enjoy in riper years. It appeared to me that there was nothing good on earth. Those things in which I had expected to find some solid good had deceived me. I began to think man was no more than a brute, and the idea of hereafter was a dream; annihilation was a chilling thought; and accountability was sure destruction to all. The heavens were as brass over my head, and the earth as iron under my feet."

Whether he was working in the hayfields or hoeing in his garden, he could not escape from his tormenting thoughts.

"Eternity!" he cried, "*what was it? And death, why was it?* The more I reasoned, the further I was from demonstration. The more I thought, the more scattered were my conclusions. I tried to stop thinking, but my thoughts would not be controlled. I was truly wretched; but did not understand the cause. I murmured and complained, but knew not of whom. I felt there was a wrong, but knew not how or where to find the right. I mourned, but without hope." [1]

It sometimes happens that a drastic statement will stir a sense of opposition in the listener that is salutary, and this occurred in a conversation he had with an acquaintance of his — Judge Stanley by name, who was evidently a confirmed deist.

"I asked him his opinion respecting our condition in another state," Miller says in his "Memoirs." "He replied

[1] J. V. Himes, *Memoirs.* Published 1841.

WILLIAM MILLER'S HOME AT LOW HAMPTON, N.Y.

by comparing it to that of a tree, which flourishes for a time and turns to earth; and to that of a candle, which burns to nothing. I was then satisfied that deism was inseparably connected with, and did tend to the denial of a future existence. And I thought to myself that rather than embrace such a view I should prefer the heaven and hell of the Scriptures, and take my chance respecting them."

This condition of mind lasted for some time and caused acute suffering. Just when all seemed darkest to him, however, a light broke in upon his misery. It happened in the little Baptist Church at Low Hampton, and he gives the following account of it:

"Suddenly," he says, "the character of a Saviour was vividly impressed upon my mind. It seemed to me that there might be a Being so good and compassionate as to atone for our transgressions, and thereby save us from suffering the penalty of sin. I immediately felt how lovely such a Being must be, and imagined that I could cast myself into the arms of, and trust in the mercy of such a One. I saw that the Bible did bring to view just such a Saviour as I needed. I was constrained to admit that the Scriptures must be a revelation from God. They became a delight," he goes on to say, "and in Jesus I found a friend. The Saviour became to me the chiefest among ten thousand; — and the Scriptures, which before were dark and contradictory, now became the lamp to my feet, and light to my path. My mind became settled and satisfied. I found the Lord God to be a rock in the ocean of life."

With what prayers of thanksgiving did Lucy Miller watch her husband coming out from the valley of shadows where he had suffered the poignant suffering of spiritual and mental conflict!

"The Bible now became my chief study," he goes on to explain, "and I can truly say I searched it with great delight. I found the half was never told me. I wondered why I had not seen its beauty and glory before, and marvelled that I could have ever rejected it. I found everything revealed that my heart could desire, and a remedy for every disease of the soul. I lost all taste for other reading, and applied my heart to get wisdom from God."

Every other thought was now subservient to this one great, absorbing question of immortality, and the assurances he found expressed in the Bible regarding it. But in studying this book of revelation, he refused to be guided by the great weight of opinion that has accumulated through the centuries, nor would he accept the interpretations given by a long line of enlightened minds to some of the obscurer passages. He decided to be his own interpreter.

According to his biographer (Sylvester Bliss),[1] "he resolved to lay aside all preconceived opinions and he received with childlike simplicity the natural and obvious meaning of Scripture. He pursued the study of the Bible," we are told, "with the most intense interest, whole nights as well as days being devoted to that object. At times delighted with truth, which shone forth from the sacred volume, making clear to his understanding the great plan of God for the redemption of fallen man; and at times puzzled and almost distracted by seemingly inexplicable or contradictory passages, he per-

[1] Elder Sylvester Bliss was a member of the Historical and Genealogical Societies of Boston, Mass.

severed until the application of his great principle in interpretation was triumphant. He became puzzled only to be delighted, and delighted only to persevere the more in penetrating its beauties and mysteries."

It caused a tremendous stir among his friends and former associates in Poultney when he made his change of belief known to them. "His infidel friends," his biographer says, "regarded his departure from them as the loss of a standard-bearer" — but the rejoicing among his own people was deep and sincere. He soon, however, began to specialize in his researches and to focus his attention upon the mysterious prophesies of Daniel, and strove to penetrate the symbolism of King Nebuchadnezzar's dream and to connect them with other prophecies found largely in the Old Testament. He accepted them literally, refusing to recognize the Hebrew custom of using metaphor, and it was not long before he became enmeshed in an intricate system of hypothetical periods of dates, all pointing toward the destruction of the world by fire, preceded by the Second Advent of our Lord.

For upwards of fourteen years William Miller's whole time was spent thus — working on his farm and in his leisure hours drawing up charts covered with a network of mathematical calculations, all tending to prove the accuracy of his system of interpreting the prophecies according to his own personal methods. And all these calculations showed that the year 1843 would usher in the Millennium. The more he worked out his theory, the more convinced he became of the truth of it.

"Various difficulties and objections," he states, "would

arise in my mind from time to time; certain texts would occur to me which seemed to weigh against my conclusions; and I would not present a view to others while any difficulty appeared to militate against it. I therefore continued the study of the Bible and to see if I could sustain any of these objections. My object was not merely to remove them, but I wished to see if they were valid.

"In this way I was occupied for five years — from 1818 to 1823 — in weighing the various objections which were being presented to my mind.

"With solemn conviction that such momentous events were predicted in the Scriptures to be fulfilled in so short a space of time, the question came home to me with mighty power regarding my duty to the world, in view of the evidence that had affected my own mind. If the end was so near, it was important that the world should know it."

Later he says: "The duty of presenting the evidence of the nearness of the Advent to others — which I had managed to evade while I found the shadow of an objection remaining against its truth — again came home to me with great force. I had previously only thrown out occasional hints of my views. I then began to speak more clearly to my neighbors, to ministers and others. To my astonishment I found very few who listened with any interest. Occasionally one would see the force of the evidence, but the great majority passed it by as an idle tale.

"I supposed it would call forth the opposition of the ungodly; but it never came into my mind that any Christian would oppose it. I supposed that all such would be so rejoiced, in view of the glorious prospect, that it only would be necessary to present it for them to receive it." [1]

This temporary setback depressed him not a little, but it did not last long. As time went on, this desire to give out his warning took possession of him again. He seemed to hear distinct voices telling him to go out and make his discovery known to the world.

"When I was about my business," he writes, "it was constantly ringing in my ears — 'Go and tell the world of their danger.' ... I felt that if the wicked could be effectually warned multitudes of them would repent." But in spite of a peculiar assurance in regard to his convictions, William Miller was a diffident man in many respects. Though he had formerly freely indulged in ridiculing others, he shrank from the shafts of it himself, and he dreaded criticism, and feared being misunderstood.

"I did all I could," he states, "to avoid the conviction that anything was required of me; and I thought that by freely speaking of it to all I should perform my duty; but still it was impressed upon me, 'Go tell it to the world.'

"The more I presented it in conversation, the more dissatisfied I felt with myself for withholding it from the public. I tried to excuse myself to the Lord for not going out and proclaiming it to the world. I told the Lord that I was not used to public speaking; that I had not the necessary qualifications for gaining the attention of an audience; that I was very diffident, and feared to go before the world; that I was slow of speech and of a slow tongue. But I could get no relief."

[1] Sylvester Bliss, *Life of William Miller*.

According to his own accounts, he resisted these inward promptings for nine years more. He was fifty years old by then, and his life of constant mental struggle and physical labor, together with the lasting effects of his illness contracted in the Army, had aged him beyond his years, and he appeared much older than he was. He was inclined to be over-stout and he felt the effort of making unusual exertion.

It was in the autumn of 1831, however, that he finally started his lecturing, and it came about in this way:

After breakfast one Saturday morning, he was sitting down to work upon his calculations of Jewish time and to review his interpretation of the prophecies when a voice seemed to say to him louder than he had ever heard it before — "Go tell it to the world!"

"The impression was so sudden," he writes, "and came with such force that I settled down in my chair, saying, 'I can't go, Lord.' 'Why not?' seemed to be the response; and then all my excuses came up — my want of ability, etc.; but my distress became so great I entered into a solemn compact with God that if He would open the way I would go and perform my duty to the world. 'What do you mean by opening the way?' seemed to come to me. 'Why,' I said, 'if I should have an invitation to speak publicly in any place, I will go tell them what I find in the Bible about the Lord's coming.' Instantly all my burden was gone, and I rejoiced that I should not probably be called upon, for I had never had such an invitation."

About half an hour after this, so he states, a young man called at the door. He was the son of a Mr. Gifford, of Dresden. He explained that there was no preacher to fill the pulpit of the church there the next day, and such being the case his father had thought it would be a fine opportunity for the congregation to hear Mr. Miller's views on the near approach of the Second Advent and the attending destruction of the world, and sent him to ask if he would come and give a lecture on the subject.

It came as a great shock to William Miller. He found himself regretting his compact with God, but he felt bound by it, and sent back the answer that he would come. It was his first experience of the kind, and he was too much agitated to make any real preparation. As he mounted the steps of the pulpit the following morning, he felt almost unequal to filling his part of the compact. Standing before the little Baptist congregation at Dresden, he hesitated for a brief moment and then he began to speak. Immediately it seemed to him that a new talent was born in him of which he had never been conscious before. As he explained his reasons for believing in the near approach of the Day of Judgment — as he pictured the sudden appearance in the heavens of the Saviour in clouds of glory, which they must be prepared to watch for any time between 1843 and 1844 — when he found a sudden flow of words to depict the consternation and confusion of the wicked — their unavailing cries for mercy — the earth shrivelling in flames — the victorious shouts of the redeemed while being caught up into the air, safe from the fiery destruction beneath them — his listeners sat upright in their pews as though spellbound.

As a spark from a passing engine is sufficient to start a forest fire, so William Miller's first lecture in the little Baptist Church at Dresden started a conflagration that the opposing clergy of the Orthodox churches, the newspapers, lecturers, and the more normal and sane-minded of the public could not quell.

After this the country folk flocked from the neighboring villages, curiosity bringing them at first, but as the news of his prophecy spread a revival commenced, accompanied by great enthusiasm, and "in thirteen families all but two were happily converted" according to the accounts of the time.

Immediately invitations came pouring in to him to lecture at various places. The town of Paulet came next, and after that it was one continual travel from place to place. In writing of this time he says:

"The churches of the Congregationalists, Baptists, and Methodists were thrown open. In almost every place I visited, my labors resulted in the reclaiming of backsliders and the conversion of sinners. I was usually invited to fields of labor by the ministers of the several congregations whom I visited, who gave me their countenance, and I have never labored in any place to which I was not previously invited. The pressing invitations from the ministry and the leading members of the churches poured in continually from that time during the whole period of my public labors, and with more than one half of which I was unable to comply. I lectured to crowded houses through the western part of Vermont, through the northern part of New York, and in Canada East."

By now he had acquired an unerring capacity for claiming the attention of his listeners at all times, and he gave the following advice to Elder Hendryx, a Baptist friend of his who had evidently written asking the secret of this art: "One great means of doing good," Miller explains in answer, "is to make your parishioners sensible that you are in earnest, and *fully* and *solemnly believe* what you preach. If you wish your people to *feel, feel yourself.* If you wish them to believe as you do, show them, by your constant assiduity in teaching, that you sincerely wish it."

The following year requests that he should publish his views began to reach him. As usual, he wrote to Elder Hendryx on the subject. His letter is dated January 23, 1832: "I have written a few numbers on the coming of Christ and the final destruction of the Beast, when his body shall be given to the burning flame. They may appear in the 'Vermont Telegraph'; — if not, in pamphlet form. They are written to Elder Smith, of Poultney, and he has liberty to publish."

By this time William Miller had acquired a style and manner of preaching that gave his sense of dramatic values free rein. This can be seen in a letter which he wrote to Elder Hendryx, dated May 30, 1832:

"I am satisfied that the end of the world is at hand. The evidence flows in from every quarter. — 'The earth is reeling to and fro like a drunkard.' ... Is the harvest over and past? If so, soon, very soon, God will arise in his anger, and the vine of the earth will be reaped. *See! See!* — the angel with his sharp sickle is about to take the field! See yonder trembling victim fall before his pestilential breath! High and low, rich and poor, trembling and falling before the appalling grave, the dreadful cholera.

"Hark! — hear those dreadful bellowings of the angry nations! It is the presage of horrid and terrific war. Look! —

look again! See crowns, and kings, and kingdoms trembling to the dust! See lords and nobles, captains and mighty men, all arming for the bloody, demon fight! See the carnivorous fowls fly screaming through the air! *See* — see these signs! Behold, the heavens grow black with clouds; the sun has veiled himself; the moon, pale and forsaken, hangs in middle air; the hail descends; the seven thunders utter loud their voices; the lightnings send their vivid gleams of sulphurous flames abroad; and the great city of the nations falls to rise no more forever and forever! At this dread moment, look! The clouds have burst asunder; the heavens appear; the great white throne is in sight! Amazement fills the Universe with awe! He comes! — He comes! — Behold the Saviour comes! — Lift up your heads, ye saints — He comes! He comes! He comes!

"WILLIAM MILLER."

One can easily see why the little Baptist congregation at Dresden sat spellbound!

Now Brother Hendryx delighted in a letter of this kind with a good revivalist flavor to it, and this was one reason why William Miller found a special enjoyment in his society. During the following March he wrote again to him and expressed himself thus: "I want to see you more than ever, and when we have less company, so that we can sit down and have a good dish of Bible together. The light is continually breaking in, and I am more and more confirmed in those things which I told you."

He then goes on in a chatty sort of way to give him the local news, an item of it being that a pastor was needed for

LAST DAY TOKENS

the church at Low Hampton and that every one was expressing himself freely as to the kind of a man most fitted for the place. "Some of our people want '*a quick gab*,'" he writes. "But I should prefer a *quick understanding!*"

Now it was about this time that strange signs appeared in the heavens and with such frequency as to cause great uneasiness. They were the precursors of the famous phenomenon of the falling stars of 1833 which produced terror and consternation among those who had heard of William Miller's prophecy. As it was, these precursors of that phenomenon were causing much comment not only from the general public, but scientific men were watching them with unusual interest.

The author was fortunate enough to find a quaint account of one of these appearances in an old Shaker journal written at that time. It reads as follows:

"Remarkable lights seen at the Second Family — Watervliet, December 2d, 1831.

"On Saturday night, December 2d, just after I retired, being still awake and looking towards the wash house, I saw it was on fire as I thought. I called to Asaneth Harwood to come and see what the matter was. She came, and on seeing the same, she said, 'Oh — that is spiritual light!' Then two Sisters got up and came to the window and saw the same. One of them told me I had better call up the Sisters in the front room, 'for it may be fire,' said she.

"I went and called up Polly Bacon and Ellen Brandet. They looked out and thought the South House barns were on fire.

"Polly then went and called up Joel Smith to go and see if

the barns were really on fire. While Joel was dressing, we kneeled and prayed that if it was a fire it might be put out.

"Then I went into the hall and met William Seeley and asked him to go and see. He went, but neither he nor Joel could see anything of the light or fire.

"I saw two large lights — then there appeared to be two dozen large sheets of light; then they all appeared to turn into little stars spreading out to great extent; and then they would seem to be gone, except the two large lights which remained when all the rest were gone. The stars would then appear again.

"I went to bed and laid as much as an hour, and saw them all the time. I fell asleep, woke again, and saw then the same as before.

"After laying awake some considerable time, I again fell asleep, and when I awoke they had disappeared.

    [Signed]            "PERMILIA EARLS."


"Note: Permilia further said that it appeared as though the light gathered into sheets that came up one behind another. When they had gathered up in this way, one large star would shoot out to the west, and then a great many would shoot upward like sparks from a blacksmith's chimney.

"Then they would collect again as before, and shoot out again in like manner, repeating the same a great many times.

"The light was of a silvery color. The other Sisters say it appeared to them in the same manner.

"Permilia also says that as she closed her eyes it appeared to her that somebody came and brushed them open two or three times, and then the room was filled with lights."

It was two years after this, and just when the belief in William Miller's prophecy was rapidly gaining ground, that the night skies to all appearances began to fall to earth. Nothing could have happened so to promote the acceptance of his prophetic calculations as the awe-inspiring sight of this strange phenomenon. The newspapers were full of it and speculated upon the causes at length.

"Surely," people exclaimed, "the prophecies of the Bible are being fulfilled! These are the signs in the heavens spoken of!" — and many trembled with fear. Some of the accounts that appeared in the newspapers are so extraordinary and reveal so clearly the tenor of the public mind at that time that a few of them must be included in the next chapter.

# CHAPTER III

## SIGNS IN THE HEAVENS

"Nature in wild amaze
Her dissolution mourns;
Blushes of blood the moon deface,
The sun to darkness turns."
*Old camp-meeting hymn*

MAN is used to looking up at the starry firmament with confidence and a sense of boundless security. He watches the planets rise and set. He knows where to look for the glittering group of the Pleiades, and for the pointed angles of Cassiopea's Chair. He can rely upon finding the exact position of the North Star, and knows the hour to watch for the Constellation of Orion. When, therefore, some time before dawn on November 13, 1833, thousands upon thousands of brilliant stars were seen falling northward and southward toward the earth, and strange, shimmering lights shot upward against the background of a cloudless sky, and balls of fire blazed in the zenith and exploded in the air, it can hardly cause astonishment that intense alarm was felt in many places. With acute concern some recalled another agitating demonstration of Nature's power which had occurred fifty years before and was recorded by scientists as the "Dark Day," when the sun, to all appearances, neither rose nor set, and darkness covered the earth, as in the nebulous days before light was. Linking that terrifying event with the present one, many hurriedly searched the Scriptures, comparing what they found there with what was

THE FAMOUS PHENOMENON OF THE FALLING STARS IN 1833

happening in the skies above them, and they tremblingly believed that the hour had come when one of the Biblical prophecies was being fulfilled right before their eyes. Throughout the districts where William Miller had been sounding the alarm of approaching doom, the excitement was intense, and wherever his word had spread, this awe-inspiring spectacle produced a profound sensation, and brought many heretofore scoffers to join those who believed in his prophecy.

The following letter addressed to the editor appeared in the "Baltimore Patriot" of November 13, 1833, and gives a vivid account of this famous phenomenon:

"Mr. Munro:

"Being up this morning, I witnessed one of the most grand and alarming spectacles which ever beamed upon the eye of Man. The light in my room was so great that I could see the hour of the morning by my watch, which hung over the mantle, and supposing that there was a fire near at hand, probably on my own premises, I sprang to the window and, behold, the stars, or some other bodies presenting a fiery appearance, were descending in torrents as rapid and numerous as ever I saw flakes of snow or drops of rain in the midst of a storm.

"Occasionally a large body of apparent fire would be hurled through the atmosphere which without noise exploded, when millions of fiery particles would be cast through the surrounding air. To the eye it presented the appearance of what might be called a raining of fire, for I can compare it to nothing else. Its continuance, according to my time from the moment I discovered it, was twenty minutes, but a friend, whose lady was up, says it commenced at half-past four — that she was watching the sick-bed of a relative and therefore can speak positively as to the hour of its commencement. If our time was correct, it rained fire fifty minutes. The shed in the yard adjoining my own was covered with stars, as I supposed, during the whole time.

"A friend at my elbow who also witnessed it, and in whose veracity I can place the most implicit reliance, confirms my own observation of the phenomenon, and adds that the fiery particles which fell south descended in a southern direction, and those north took a northern direction. He thinks it commenced earlier than at the period at which I first witnessed it, and that it lasted longer — that when the clock struck six there were still occasional descents of stars.

"I have stated facts as they present themselves to my mind. I leave it to the philosophers to account for the phenomenon.

"Yours truly

"'B.'"

Startling as this description is, there are many others written at the time that are equal to it. Henry Dana Ward's account, sent to the "New York Chamber of Commerce," is one of them. He writes as follows:

"In your paper this morning some notice is taken of the phenomenon of yesterday. It comes so far short of the view taken of it by myself, and a number of friends who gazed upon it with me, that I send you the story of that eventful scene, as we witnessed it.

"One of the family rose at five o'clock A.M. to prepare for leaving the city in the seven o'clock boat. He threw up the window to see whether the dawn had come, and behold! the east was lighted up and the heavens were apparently falling. He rubbed his eyes in doubt, but seeing on every side the starry firmament as it were broken up and falling like flakes of snow and whitening the skies, he aroused the whole family. At the cry, 'Look out of the window!' I sprang from a deep sleep, and with wonder saw the east lighted up with the dawn of meteors.

"The zenith, the north, and the west also showed the falling stars in the very image of one thing and of only one I ever heard of. I called to my wife to behold, and while robing she exclaimed, 'See how the stars fall!' — and we felt in our hearts that it was the sign of the last days. For truly 'the stars of Heaven fall onto the earth, even as a fig tree casteth her untimely figs when she is shaken by a mighty wind.'"

This same idea was expressed in an article in the "Connecticut Observer," of November 25, 1833, which was copied from a paper called the "Old Countryman." It reads as follows:

"We pronounce the raining of fire which we saw on Wednesday morning last, an awful type, a sure forerunner — a merciful sign of the great and dreadful day which the inhabitants of the earth will witness when the Sixth Seal shall be opened. The time is just at hand described, not only in the New Testament, but in the Old. A more correct picture of a fig tree casting its leaves when blown by a mighty wind is not possible to behold."

A correspondent of the "New York American" at Acquackanonk seems to have had a peculiarly trying experience. He states that the shooting stars varied in size from the bulk of a pea to that of a walnut, and were varied in colors — red, blue, yellow, and white! "Several," he writes, "came within a foot of the writer's person, and one *exploded close to his face, and instantaneously disappeared without any particular odor!*"

In a publication called "Last Day Tokens" (1843) several newspaper reports of this phenomenon of the falling stars were reprinted, one of which reads thus:

"The Sussex papers described the exhibition in their vicinity as having been somewhat singular. The people seem to have been much alarmed. They thought that the stars had in reality shot madly from their spheres, and that the whole economy of Nature was returning to its original chaos. One person said that *he kept his eye upon the morning star*, resolved that if that departed he should give up all hope!"

The "Rockingham (Virginia) Register" called it "a rain of fires — thousands of stars being seen falling at once; — some said it began with considerable noise!"

The "Lancaster Examiner" declared that "the air was filled with innumerable meteors or stars — hundreds of thousands of brilliant bodies might be seen falling at every moment."

The "Salem Register" stated that "some attributed them to stones ejected by volcanoes on the moon."

THE RAIN OF FIRE, OR FALLING STARS, OF 1833

After these graphic accounts it is interesting to note the opinion of a scientist. In commenting upon the extraordinary spectacle, Professor Olmstead, of Yale College, made the following statement, according to the aforesaid paper, "Last Day Tokens" (1843):

"Those who were so fortunate as to witness the exhibition of shooting stars on the morning of November 13, 1833, probably saw the greatest display of celestial fireworks that has ever been seen since the creation of the world, or at least within the annals covered by the pages of history."

After this, as his following grew in numbers, William Miller's enthusiasm and faith in his own prophecy increased accordingly. In a letter to good Brother Hendryx that same year he burst forth into a Walt Whitman-like flow of language that is bewildering. Yet this style was peculiarly his own and the following is an interesting example of it:

"I wish I had the tongue of an Apollo, and the mental powers of a Paul!" he writes in this exuberant letter. "O may the Bible be to us a rock, a pillar, a compass, a chart, a statute, a directory, a polar star, a traveller's guide, a pilgrim's companion, a shield of faith, a ground of hope, a history, a chronology, an armory, a storehouse, a mirror, a toilet, a closet, a prayer-book, an epistle, a love letter, a friend, a foe, a revenue, a treasury, a bank, a fountain, a cistern, a garden, a lodge, a field, a haven, a sun, a moon, a star, a door, a window, a light, a lamp, a luminary, a morning, a noon, an evening, an hour-glass, a dayman, a servant, a handmaid!

"It is meat, food, drink, raiment, shelter, warmth, heat,

a feast, fruit, apples, pictures, wine, milk, honey, bread, butter, oil, refreshment, rest, strength, stability, wisdom, life, eyes, hands, feet, breath; it is a help to hearing, seeing, feeling, tasting, smelling, understanding, forgiving, loving, hoping, enjoying, adoring, and saving; it teaches salvation, justification, sanctification, redemption and glorification; it declares condemnation, destruction and desolation; it tells us what we were, are, and shall be; begins with the beginning, carries us through the intermediate and ends only with the end; it is past, present, and to come; it discourses the first great cause of all effects, and the effects of all causes; it speaks of life, death, and judgment, body, soul, and spirit, heaven, earth, and hell; it makes use of all nature as figures, to sum up the value of the gospel; and declares itself to be the word of God. And your friend and brother believes it.

"WILLIAM MILLER."

But he had to suffer for this change of faith. His former associates were indignant at it. They termed it an audacity for him to be preaching to others what he had denied as a fallacy in the past. Other friends, remembering his scathing ridicule of themselves and their faith in former days, could not resist casting his own taunts back into his face.

From this he suffered keenly, and at times he felt his courage sorely tried. Like many who indulge in casting ridicule upon the religious faith of others, he felt the sting of it to be almost beyond endurance when he found it turned upon himself. But he was too deeply in earnest to be led into swerving away from the path he was now following, and he continued to plod from place to place, carrying his message and sounding his warning.

The Baptist Church had by this time accorded him a license to preach and in a letter to Brother Hendryx dated February 23, 1834, he refers to this:

"You have undoubtedly heard that I have been trying to *preach* (as some call it) about in this vicinity (Low Hampton). I have been laboring, it is true, in my weak manner, in Dresden two or three months. . . . You laugh, Bro. Hendryx, to think old Bro. Miller is preaching! But laugh on: You are not the only one that laughs; and it is all right. I deserve it. If I could preach the truth, it is all I could ask."

In reply to a letter addressed to him as Reverend he again writes to Brother Hendryx:

"DEAR BRO. HENDRYX:

"I wish you would look into your Bible and see if you can find the word Rev. applied to a sinful mortal like myself, and govern yourself accordingly. . . . Let us be determined to live and die on the Bible. God is about to arise and punish the inhabitants of the world. The proud, the high, the lofty must be brought low; and the humble, the meek, and the contrite be exalted. Then, what care I for what the world calls great and honorable? Give me Jesus, and a knowledge of his word, faith in his name, hope in his grace, interest in his love, and let me be clothed in his righteousness, and the world may enjoy all the high-sounding titles, the riches it can boast, the vanities it is heir to, and all the pleasures of sin; and they will be no more than a drop in the ocean."

Again he writes:

"After haying and harvesting are over, I shall go forth again. If I am correct, how important is time! Nine years will pass soon; and then, dear brother, you and I must render our account before the solemn bar of our omnipotent Judge."

Evidently Brother Hendryx, while agreeing with his friend's views on many points did not wholly subscribe to his belief in the coming destruction of the world, and this was a source of great trouble to William Miller; in fact, this attitude of neutrality on his part and on the part of many others of the clergy regarding the subject was one that tried his patience exceedingly.

"The evidence is so clear," he writes to him on October 28, 1834, "the testimony is so strong that we live on the eve of the present dispensation, towards the dawn of the *Glorious Day*, that I wonder why ministers and people do not wake up and trim their lamps. Yes, my brother, almost two years since you heard the news, 'Behold the bridegroom cometh!' — and yet you cry, 'A little more sleep, a little more slumber.' Blame not your people if they go to sleep under your preaching. You have done the same. Bear with me, my brother. In every letter you have written me you have promised to study this all-important subject, and in every letter you confess your negligence. The day draws near. More than one sixth of the time is gone since my Brother Hendryx promised, and is yet asleep! Oh, God, forgive him! Are you waiting for all the world to wake up, before you get up? 'Where has your courage fled?' Awake! Awake! O Sluggard! Defend your own castle, or take sides those intricate calculations that brought out the startling deduction that some time between 1843 and 1844 the world would be destroyed by fire.

This natural and unstudied manner of speaking out his thoughts as they came to him, without hesitation and according to his mood, instilled pulsating life into the long explanatory lectures he was now being called upon to deliver, day after day, almost without cessation.

The following February (1835) he wrote again to Brother Hendryx:

"The Lord opens doors faster than I can fill them. To-morrow I have an appointment at Whiting which will occupy a week. The next week I shall be in Shoreham; the last week in this month at Bridgeport; the first week in March in Middletown, the second in Hoosac. I have calls from Schroon, Ticonderoga, Moriah, Essex, Chazy, Champlain, Plattsburg, Peru, Mooretown, Canton, Pottsdam, Hopkinton, Stockholm, Parishville, and other places too numerous to mention."

The result of these lectures was a formal announcement made by a large number of Baptist clergymen to this effect:

"This may certify, to whom it may concern, that we whose names are hereunto affixed — being ministers in the denomination of regular Baptists — are personally acquainted with Bro. William Miller, the bearer of this certificate; that he is a member, and licentiate in good regular standing, in the particular Baptist Church, in Hampton, N.Y.; that we have heard him lecture on the subject of the Second Coming and Reign of our Lord Jesus Christ; and that we believe his views on that particular subject, as well

as others pertaining to the Gospel, are worthy to be known
and read of all men. . . .

> [Signed]  "J. SAWYER, JR., South Reading
> "E. HALPING, Hampton
> "AMOS STEARNS, Fort Ann
> "EMERSON ANDREWS, Lansingburgh."

Below this is written: "Having heard the above-men-
tioned lectures, I see no way to avoid the conclusion that the
coming of Christ will be as soon as 1843." And to this is
affixed a list of thirty-eight names of men from New York,
Vermont, and Massachusetts.

His public lectures during the winter of 1835 were inter-
rupted by his preparation of sixteen lectures which were
published the following spring in Troy, New York, by
Elder Wescott, with the arrangement that the copies held by
William Miller should be purchased by him at the market
price. The desire to reach broader fields and to spread his
doctrine among all classes was so great that when the prop-
osition was made to him, he accepted it eagerly. The
public accused him of trying to reap a fortune from his
publication, being ignorant of the terms made concerning it.

The following summer his friend Brother Hendryx received another letter from him dated July 21st.

"I have been confined at home for three weeks past by a
bilious complaint," he writes. "I was taken unwell while
lecturing at Lansingburg, N.Y., but I finished my course of
lectures and returned home, and have not been well since.
My lectures were well received in that place and excited
attention. The house was filled to overflowing for eight

A STRANGE PHENOMENON IN THE HEAVENS CALLED PARHELIA

Seen in February, 1843

days in succession. I feel that God was there, and believe that in His glorified kingdom I shall see the fruits. . . . Infidels, deists, Universalists, and sectarians were all chained to their seats in perfect silence for hours — yes, days — to hear the old stammering man talk about the Second Coming of Christ, and show the manner, object, time, and signs of His Coming."

That a distinct uneasiness and apprehension regarding the prediction of the approach of the Second Advent troubled the public mind was strikingly apparent from the fact that while Prophet Miller was lecturing to great crowds in the smaller towns and rural districts upon his interpretation of the prophecies, Harriet Livermore, who viewed the manner and object of the coming of our Saviour from a totally different standpoint, was preaching in the Hall of Congress in Washington before President Madison and many of his Cabinet, and a vast concourse of people. Moreover, a new prophet had arisen in England, a Captain Saunders, of Liverpool, who was predicting the Second Advent would occur in 1847, agreeing with Joseph Wolff, who was awaiting it in Jerusalem. From this time on Prophet Miller labored incessantly, delivering as many as eighty-two lectures in the fall of 1836. People were now beginning publicly to acknowledge themselves as his followers, and an incident of this sort happened when he visited Shaftsbury, Vermont, on January 23, 1837, where he gave his full course of sixteen lectures.

"At the close of one lecture a Baptist clergyman arose and stated that he had come there for the purpose of exposing the folly of Mr. M., but he had to confess that he was confounded, convicted, and converted. He acknowledged that he had applied various unhandsome appellations to Mr. Miller, calling him 'the end of the world man' — 'the old visionary' — 'dreamer' — 'fanatic,' and for which he felt covered with shame and confusion. That confession, evidently so honest, was like a thunderbolt on the audience." [1]

No sooner did he lecture in one town or village now than all the neighboring towns and villages wished to hear him, and space does not admit of the long list of places covering a wide territory where he gave forth his solemn warning to the bewildered inhabitants.

He had little time for farming in these days — all his strength was given to what he considered to be his mission.

His family now consisted of a wife and ten children — seven sons and three daughters; some of them grown up by this time and able to care for the farm. Little reference is made to them in his biography, but he frequently wrote to his eldest son, and one of his letters, written to him on November 17, 1838, from Montpelier, Vermont, shows how the agitation produced by the nature of his prophecy was taking hold of the imagination of the public.

"There was great excitement on the subject in this place," he states. "Last night we had a solemn and interesting meeting. There was a great breaking down and much weeping. Some souls have been born again. I can hardly get away from these people. They want me to stay another week. . . . Montpelier is quite a considerable village, and contains some very intelligent people who appear to listen with much interest. This afternoon I meet the citizens, and am to give

[1] Sylvester Bliss, *Life of William Miller.*

them an opportunity to ask questions and state objections. .... May God help me to give His truth! I know my own weakness, and I know that I have neither body nor mind to do what the Lord is doing by me. It is the Lord's doings and marvellous in our eyes. The world does not know how weak I am. They think much more of the old man than I think of him."

Again he writes to him in January, 1839:

"There has been a reformation in every place I have lectured in since I left home, and the work is progressing in every place rapidly. The meeting-houses are crowded to overflowing. Much excitement prevails amongst the people. Many say they believe; some scoff; others are sober and thinking."

There is a quaint description of William Miller as he appeared at this period which is worth mentioning. Elder T. Cole, pastor of the Baptist Church at Lowell, had been hearing of the great revivals that resulted from Prophet Miller's lectures as he travelled through the State of Vermont, and he, as well as the people of Lowell, was exceedingly curious to see him, and to find out what he had to say on the subject of his prophecy. Accordingly he wrote a letter to him urging him to come to Massachusetts and to stop at Lowell and explain his doctrine from the pulpit of the Baptist Church. Evidently Elder Cole had formed a very definite picture of him in his mind and looked forward to seeing a commanding figure, such as could sway the emotions of a crowd through the force of his personality. Now William Miller was in reality a perfectly simple and unpretentious sort of man, in many ways very ingenuous, and probably never gave as much as a thought to his personal appearance. He was very plain and ordinary in his dress, being attired more as a farmer would be than as a preacher. Elder Cole seems to have expected him to look "like some distinguished doctor of divinity," according to Miller's biographer, and though he had heard that he always wore a camlet cloak and a shaggy white beaver hat, he apparently assumed they would be made according to the fashion of the times.

When the day came for him to arrive at Lowell, the Elder went to the station to meet him. He carefully inspected each person that alighted from the train, but he saw no one that answered to his mental picture of Prophet Miller. Soon he saw an old man, shaking with palsy, with a white hat and camlet cloak alight from the cars. Fearing that this might prove to be the man, and, if so, regretting that he had invited him to lecture in his church, he stepped up and whispered in his ear, "Is your name Miller?" Mr. M. nodded in assent. "Well," said Elder Cole very much disturbed, "follow me."

"He led the way, walking ahead, and Mr. M. keeping as near as he could till he reached his house. He was much chagrined that he had written for a man of Mr. M.'s appearance, who, he concluded, could know nothing respecting the Bible, but would confine his discourse to visions and fancies of his own. After tea he told Mr. M. he supposed it was about time to attend church, and again led the way, Mr. M. bringing up the rear. When they entered the church he showed him to the desk and he himself sat with the congregation.

SOLAR HALOES SEEN IN DANVILLE, KY.,
JANUARY 4, 1843

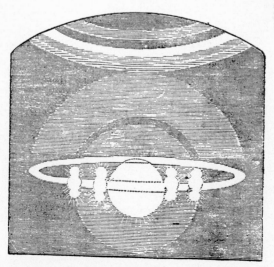

SOLAR HALOES AND PARHELIA SEEN IN NEW
YORK, SEPTEMBER 9, 1844

"Fifteen minutes after the text had been given out, Elder Cole was wholly disarmed. On that occasion William Miller spoke quietly and impressively, and the arguments he put forth seemed so convincing that he was urged to stay and lecture at greater length to the people. This ended in 'a glorious revival' and Elder Cole embraced his views in full, continuing for six years a devoted advocate of them." [1]

From Lowell he went to Groton and from there to Lynn, and a memorandum in his diary states that from October 1, 1834, to June 9, 1839, he delivered eight hundred lectures.

The editor of the "Lynn Record" wrote an article which appeared in that paper immediately after William Miller had lectured in that place. It was named "Miller and his Prophecies," and it also gives a description of him which is interesting. It reads as follows:

"We took a prejudice against the good man when he first came among us, on account of what we supposed a glaring error in interpreting the Scripture prophecies so that the world would come to an end in 1843. We are still inclined to believe this an error or miscalculation. At the same time we have overcome our prejudice against him by attending his lectures, and learning more of the excellent character of this man, and of the great good he has done, and is doing. Mr. Miller is a plain farmer, and pretends to nothing except that he has made the Scripture prophecies an intense study for many years, understands some of these differently from most people, and wishes for the good of others to spread his views before the public. No one can hear him five minutes without being convinced of his sincerity, and instructed by

[1] Sylvester Bliss, *Life of William Miller*.

his reasoning and information. All acknowledge his lectures to be replete with useful and interesting matter. His knowledge of the Scriptures is very extensive and minute — that of the prophecies especially, surprisingly familiar. We have reason to believe that the preaching or lecturing of Mr. Miller has been productive of great and extensive good. Revivals have been following in his train. He has been heard with attention wherever he has been.

"There is nothing very peculiar in the manner and appearance of Mr. Miller. His gestures are easy and expressive, and his personal appearance every way decorous. His Scripture explanations and illustrations are strikingly simple, natural, and forcible, and the great eagerness of the people to hear him has been manifest wherever he has preached."

Evidently the editor of the "Lynn Record" felt differently from Elder Cole in regard to the camlet cloak and white beaver hat! But the personal appearance of William Miller, rough and old-fashioned or otherwise, seems to have made no difference, for wherever he went the crowd gathered to listen to him. He wrote to his son after lecturing at Stoughton and then going on to Canton to this effect: "Lectured *three times* on the last day to a house jammed full!" — and so it was at one place after another.

Then came a change — Prophet Miller was no longer to be a roaming country preacher. Destiny had something else in store for him. He was suddenly to find himself facing the sophisticated crowds of big cities — to be challenged by the pulpit and press regarding his belief, to be surrounded by followers and detractors, friends and enemies, believers and scoffers.

This great change began the twelfth day of November, 1840, when he chanced to meet the Reverend Joshua V. Himes, a man of indomitable energy, who took Prophet Miller out from the simple, peaceful, rural districts and placed him in the lime-light of city thoroughfares, there to sound his note of warning above the din of countless noises and the clamor of innumerable voices.

It will be seen how this change was like sowing the wind and reaping the whirlwind as regards the simple-minded old prophet, who was fast ageing under the stress of the situation he had created, and that now threatened to overwhelm him.

# CHAPTER IV

## SPREADING THE WARNING

"That awful day will surely come,
Th' appointed hour makes haste."
From *The Millennial Harp*
(Published by Joshua V. Himes, 1843)

IT happened this way: The Reverend Joshua V. Himes was pastor of the Chardon Street Baptist Chapel in Boston. It has been said that he had been a Unitarian minister before he became a Baptist. However that may be, he was a very complex character, and whether it was a fortunate or unfortunate day for William Miller when the two met is hard to say. But at least it may be said that it was fortunate for succeeding generations — for had it not been for the influence he exerted over him and the publicity he gave him and his prophecy, William Miller in all probability would have remained in the rural districts; the big centres of activity would have known him only by rumor, and one of the strangest episodes in the religious history of our country would have passed by more or less unnoticed and unrecorded.

It was on this day, November 12, 1840, that Mr. Himes invited William Miller to come to Boston and lecture in the Chardon Street Chapel, and the invitation was accepted.

From the 8th to the 16th of December, Miller lectured there for the first time — Mr. Himes taking care to advertise his coming very freely. It was a good deal of a tax upon the farmer-prophet's self-possession to face the critical audiences that now sat in front of him. Throughout the

JOSHUA V. HIMES

country districts he had looked down from the lecture platform at faces upon which were engraved wonder, fear, and
credulity; but now, as he watched the expressions of those
before him, he realized that all his powers of imagery, per-
suasion, and lucid explanation must be brought to bear upon
hostile sentiments which he was fully aware were percolating through the city people who were now his listeners.

On December 12th he wrote to his son: "I am now in this
place lecturing twice a day to large audiences — many, very
many, go away unable to gain admittance. Many, I am informed, are under serious convictions. I hope God will work
in this city."

Mr. Himes had invited Mr. Miller to stay at his house
while delivering these lectures, and he was one of his most
eager listeners. It gave him an opportunity to hold many
intimate conversations alone with this man who believed
with such certainty that the Day of Doom was at hand, and
though of a quiet and sedate exterior, Mr. Himes nursed
within his breast a love of emotional crowds and religious
excitement — of revivals and camp-meetings full of exhil-
arating shouts of "Glory! Glory!" interspersed with frequent "Hallelujahs!" He was not one to thrive on monotony
in any sense of the word. Action and authority and stirring
up the public were as breath to his nostrils. A belief in
eternal damnation and hell fires, and in the wrath of an
avenging Creator, appealed to him. He always longed to see
the "sinner's bench" and the "anxious seats" full to overflowing, but he wanted the reins of control to be in his own
hands.

When he heard William Miller's lectures, they filled for

him a long-felt want; he was profoundly impressed by them, and at once accepted many of his interpretations of the Scriptural prophecies as correct, though in the depths of his mind he was not wholly convinced that the world would be destroyed in 1843. But that made no difference — he saw a great opportunity to stir sluggard Christians into a ferment of religious enthusiasm — he believed in awaking fear in the hearts of sinners, and thus bringing them to repentance. He believed also that the end justified the means, and undoubtedly believed himself to be in the right when he fanned the flames of hysterical agitation which William Miller's prophecy had ignited, and spread his doctrine far and wide. He was undoubtedly under the spell of the times, but in character he was a strange mixture of calculation and emotion — of astuteness and lack of foresight. He followed the injunction to let the future take care of itself too literally.

"When Mr. Miller had closed his lectures," he wrote, "I found myself in a new position. I could not believe or preach as I had done. Light on this subject was blazing on my conscience night and day. A long conversation with Mr. Miller then took place on our duties and responsibilities." Then came the following conversation:

"I said to Brother Miller, 'Do you really believe this doctrine?'

"He replied, 'Certainly I do, or I would not preach it.'

"'What are you doing to spread or diffuse it through the world?'

"'I have done and am still doing all I can.'

"'Well, the whole thing is kept in a corner yet. There is

but little knowledge on the subject, after all you have done. If Christ is to come in a few years, as you believe, no time should be lost in giving the church and world warning in thunder-tones, to arouse them to prepare.'

"'I know it, I know it, Brother Himes,' he said, 'but what can an old farmer do? I was never used to public speaking; I stand alone, and though I have labored much, and seen many converted to God and the truth, yet *no one* as yet seems to enter into the object and spirit of my mission, so as to render me much aid. They like to have me preach and build up their churches; and there it ends with most of the ministers as yet. I have been looking for help — I want help.'

"It was at this time I laid myself, family, society, reputation, all, upon the altar of God to help him to the extent of my power, to the end. I then inquired of him what parts of the country he had visited, and whether he had visited any of our principal cities.

"He informed me of his labors, etc. 'But why,' I said, 'have you not been into the large cities?'

"He replied that his rule was to visit those places where invited, and that he had not been invited into any of the large cities.

"'Well,' I said, 'will you go with me where doors are opened?'

"'Yes — I am ready to go anywhere, and labor to the extent of my ability to the end.'

"Then I told him he might prepare for the campaign; for doors should be opened in every city in the Union, and the warning should go to the ends of the earth.

"Here I began to help Father Miller."

This was the starting-point of the new era in William Miller's career as a prophet and a preacher. Imbued with fresh enthusiasm, he infused into his lectures a more compelling appeal than ever before to those rudderless souls that become magnetized under the spell of a powerfully directed delusion. As a demonstration of this, after a course of lectures which he delivered in Portsmouth, New Hampshire, in January, 1840, the Baptist minister, Elder David Millard, wrote in the "Christian Herald" regarding it:

"During the nine days he remained, crowds flocked to hear him. . . . Such an intense feeling as now pervaded our congregation we never witnessed before in any place. Such an awful spirit of solemnity seemed to settle down on the place that hard must be the sinner's heart that could withstand it. Yet, during the whole, not an appearance of confusion occurred; all was order and solemnity. Generally as souls found deliverance they were ready to proclaim it, and exhort their friends in moving language to come to the fountain of Life. Probably about one hundred and fifty souls have been converted in our meetings, . . . the blessed work soon spread into every congregation in town favorable to revivals. It would be difficult at present to ascertain the exact number of conversions in town — probably from five to seven hundred. For weeks together the ringing of bells for daily meetings rendered our town like a continual Sabbath. Indeed, such a season of revival was never witnessed before in Portsmouth by the oldest inhabitant. Never while we linger on the shores of mortality do we expect to enjoy more of heaven than we have in some of our late meetings and our baptism occasions. At the waterside thousands would gather to witness this solemn institution in Zion, and many would return from the place weeping." [1]

The news of the revival at Portsmouth spread like wild-fire and set all the towns agog. The Baptist churches were especially insistent that Prophet Miller should favor them by arousing their dormant congregations, but other denominations invited him also, and calls came to him from every direction. The little hill-town of Westford, near Groton, Massachusetts, secured him next, but there he was destined to receive a severe rebuff. Those who had invited him to come planned to have the lectures given in the Congregational Church, that being able to seat more persons than any other place available, but when the time came the minister refused to allow the church to be used for that purpose, which caused a tremendous excitement in the place and much protest, but he held his ground and the lectures were delivered elsewhere. This was the first rebuff of the kind that was given to Miller, and revealed the anxiety and disapproval which his opponents were beginning to feel regarding the growing excitement due to the spread of his doctrine.

Prior to this he had been looked upon by the clergy as a more or less harmless enthusiast, possessing a certain gift of appeal. The year 1843 had appeared to them like a distant speck on the horizon which lacked reality, and they did not regard his prophecy seriously. But now it was different — the time was slipping by, bringing that year, which he held to be doomed, nearer and nearer; and the prophecy was taking on the form of an actual reality. More-

[1] Sylvester Bliss, *Life of William Miller*.

over, a change had come over William Miller. When he had been alone in spreading his gospel, he had felt the lack of friends and the lack of any sustaining background, and his powers were kept somewhat in check. But the situation had suddenly changed. Behind him now stood the Reverend Joshua V. Himes — no mere shadow for opponents to contend with, but equal in his spare person to a whole congregation of any size, and in this feeling of security and this sense of receiving encouragement, all his native gift of argument and originality and his somewhat uncouth powers of oratory, combined with a sincere conviction of the truth of his premises, were let loose to the confusion of many of the orthodox clergy.

The effect of this was electrical. In October he had lectured for ten days in the near-by village of Groton, and the Congregational minister, the Reverend Silas Hawley, had written down some comments in regard to him. "Mr. Miller," he says, "has lectured in this and adjoining towns with marked success. His lectures have been succeeded by precious revivals of religion in all these places. A class of minds are reached by him not within the influence of other men. His lectures are well adapted, so far as I have learned, for shaking the supremacy of the various forms of error that are rife in the community." And now from Littleton, close by, where the lectures were given from the 19th to the 26th of December, the Baptist minister, the Reverend Oliver Ayer states: "I baptized twelve at our last Communion. I shall probably baptize from fifteen to twenty next time. There have been from thirty-five to forty hopeful conversions. There is also quite a work in Westford — ten or twelve conversions and twenty or thirty inquiries. The work is still going on."

The truth was that Prophet Miller's long and intensive study of the Bible, however erroneously he interpreted many parts of it, gave him a tremendous advantage over the general run of country clergymen, whose knowledge left much to be desired. Elder D. J. Robinson, pastor of the Methodist Church in Portsmouth, New Hampshire, had felt his personal lack of it when Miller had lectured in that place, and wrote in regard to his own position: "I heard him all I could the first week, and thought I could stop his wheels and confound him; but as the revival had commenced in the vast congregation assembled to hear him, I would not do it publicly, lest evil should follow. I therefore visited him at his room, with a formidable list of objections. To my surprise scarcely any of them were new to him, and he could answer them as fast as I could present them. And then he presented objections and questions which confounded *me* and the commentaries on which I had relied. I went home used up, convicted, humbled, and resolved to examine the questions."

The result of this was that Prophet Miller had added another convert to his list. Elder Robinson became convinced that his interpretations and calculations of time were correct and he "began to preach accordingly." [1]

Now this last statement in regard to Elder Robinson is the keynote to half of the fanaticism that wrecked so many lives and caused so much distress of mind in 1843 and 1844. With only a limited understanding of many points in Miller's doctrine, this good man and a host of others like him

[1] Sylvester Bliss, *Life of William Miller*.

took upon themselves the task of aiding the latter to spread it, and went about in every direction preaching his prophecy of the approaching destruction of the world and his religious doctrine with the addition of many theories of their own, thus increasing the confusion of thought that was beginning to be viewed with serious apprehension by the more level-headed of the public.

The Reverend Charles Fitch, pastor of the Marlborough Street Chapel in Boston, took upon himself the duty of warning the public of the coming end. By so doing he lost all connection with his church and, as he expressed it in a pamphlet he wrote in 1841, giving his reasons for believing in Miller's prophecy and which was published by Joshua V. Himes: "I became in part an ecclesiastical outcast. But I gained deliverance, in this process from the fear of man, and learned the blessedness of fearing God."

It may be instructive to insert here as a specimen a few lines of the kind of warning Brother Fitch took upon himself to give out. The following extract from a poem, entitled "The Warning," was written by him at this time and it had a wide circulation:

"THE WARNING"

"Toil on, ye grovelling worms of earth,
  Scorn and forget your heavenly birth;
  Gather your heaps of shining dust,
  And die — as soon, right soon, ye must!
  Or, if your spirit thirsts for fame,
  Make haste, nor rest, until your name
  Stands among those accounted great,
  From battle-fields, or halls of state;
  Put on your laurels for a day —
  You'll soon be swept from earth away.

If all you ask is pleasure's cup,
Haste, fill it, drink its contents up;
Fill it, if life is spared, again,
And from the brim to bottom drain,
Then drop it from your palsied hand,
And in your Maker's presence stand!
Receive your doom, and haste accursed
To dwell where your tormenting thirst
No drop of water can allay
While endless ages pass away!
No prayers, nor tears, will then avail;
Your lost and suffering spirit's wail
Forever o'er hell's burning sea
Must break in tones of agony!"

Is it any wonder that the "sinner's bench" and the "anxious seats" were becoming overcrowded at the lectures? This appalling poem hot from the pen of Brother Fitch was published after he had listened to a course of lectures given by Prophet Miller at the Chardon Street Chapel in Boston at the end of January, 1841, which place, according to his biographer, "was crowded almost to suffocation, and thousands were obliged to retire for want of room."

The doors which Elder Joshua V. Himes (as he was now called) had promised would be opened to him were opening wide now. More than that, the indefatigable Elder was publishing a paper, called "Signs of the Times," in which Miller's doctrine, and full and complete explanations of his calculations regarding the end of the world, appeared, and copies of it were sent out broadcast, regardless of cost. In reference to this afterwards William Miller wrote as follows:

"With this commenced an entire new era in the spread of information on the peculiar points of my belief. Mr. Murray gave up to him [Elder Himes] the publication of my lectures, and he published them in connection with other works on the prophecies, which aided by devoted friends he scattered broadcast everywhere to the extent of his means. I cannot here withhold my testimony to the efficiency and integrity of my Brother Himes." [1]

More than that, Elder Himes published a "Memoir of William Miller," in which volume other writings of his were included, and this also was given a wide circulation. But considering the energy and money expended, and the apparent enthusiasm with which Elder Himes spread far and wide this prophecy of the approaching end of all things according to Miller's calculations, the guarded wording of the preface written by himself is certainly surprising: — in fact, one wonders whether Miller ever read it — occupied as he was in lecturing here, there, and everywhere; but it could hardly have satisfied him if he did. The wording of it justifies the suspicion which many held regarding Elder Himes, that he approved of stirring up religious excitement at all odds.

"Notwithstanding the fears of many, esteemed wise and good, that the effect of this class of writings on the Community would be deleterious," he states, "we have, on the contrary, witnessed, as we expected, the most happy results. Their moral and religious influence upon all classes who have given them a candid examination has been most salutary. ... As it respects the general views of Mr. Miller, we consider them in the main to be in accordance with the Word of God. We do not, however, adopt the peculiarities of any man. We call no man Master. Yet we frankly avow that there is much in his theory that we approve and embrace as gospel truth.

[1] *Apology and Defense*, p. 21.

... The final destiny of the righteous and the wicked; — on all these points we fully agree with him.

"On the question of '*prophetic periods*,' and of his laborious and learned chronology, we are not competent, with our limited erudition on the subject, to decide with such positiveness as on the other topics; having never given our attention to the critical study of the subject until the last year. We, however, believe in the definiteness of *prophetic periods*, and feel satisfied that we live near the end of time. ... Some have fixed upon the year 1866, some 1847, while Mr. Miller fixes 1843 as 'the time of the end.' We think he has given the more satisfactory demonstration of the correctness of his calculation. The advent is near. It is possible we may be mistaken in the chronology. It may vary a few years, but we are persuaded the end cannot be far distant. ...

"We are not insensible of the fact that much obloquy will be cast upon us in consequence of our association with the author of this work. This, however, gives us no pain. We had rather be associated with such a man as William Miller, and stand with him in gloom or glory, in the cause of the living God, than be associated with his enemies, and enjoy all the honors of the world."

But in spite of this guarded profession of faith on the part of Elder Himes, he did his utmost to push William Miller and his prophecy to the fore. The latter, seemingly all unconscious of any lack on the part of his friend and coadjutor, lifted his voice in resounding tones with greater and greater insistence and greater and greater solemnity.

From Watertown, where he lectured for nine days, he wrote a letter to his son:

"I have never seen so great an effect in any one place as there," he states — "I preached last from Gen. 19. 17. There were from a thousand to fifteen hundred present and more than one hundred under conviction. One half of the congregation wept like children when I parted from them. Mr. Medbury, the Baptist minister — a good man — wept as though his heart would break when he took me by the hand, and, for himself and people, bade me farewell. He and many others fell upon my neck and wept and kissed me, and sorrowed most of all that they should see my face no more. We could not get away for more than an hour, and finally we had to break away."

In Portland, Maine, a number of rum shops were turned into meeting rooms by the proprietors. Some of the gambling establishments were entirely broken up, and according to Elder L. D. Fleming, the Baptist minister in that place, business men of various denominations met in offices down in the business quarter and devoted an hour in the middle of the day to prayer. "In fact," he wrote, "it would be impossible to give any adequate idea of the interest now felt in this city. There is nothing like extravagant excitement, but an almost universal solemnity on the minds of all the people. One of the principal booksellers informed me that he had sold more Bibles in one month since Mr. Miller came here than he had in four months previous."

The Maine "Wesleyan Journal" came out about that time with a description of his person and of his style of preaching, noting details that make the picture realistic, and therefore interesting. The following is an extract from it:

"Mr. Miller has been in Portland lecturing to crowded congregations in Casco Street Church, on his favorite theme, the end of the world, or literal reign of Christ for one thousand years. As faithful chroniclers of passing events it will be expected of us that we should say something of the man and his peculiar views. Mr. Miller is about sixty years of age; a plain farmer from Hampton, in the State of New York. He is a member of the Baptist Church in that place, from which he brings satisfactory testimonials of good standing and a license to preach publicly. He has, we understand, numerous testimonials also from different denominations, favorable to his general character. We should think him a man of but common school education; evidently possessing strong powers of mind, which for about fourteen years have been almost exclusively bent in the investigation of scriptural prophecies. The last eight years of his life have been devoted to lecturing on his favorite subject.

"In his public discourse he is self-possessed and ready; distinct in his utterance, and frequently quaint in his expressions. He succeeds in claiming the attention of his auditory from an hour and a half to two hours; and in the management of his subject discovers much tact — holding frequent colloquies with the objector and inquirer, supplying the questions and answers himself, sometimes producing a smile from a portion of his auditors.

"Mr. Miller is a great stickler for literal interpretations; never admitting the figurative unless absolutely required to make correct sense, or meet the events to be pointed out. He doubtless believes most unwaveringly all he teaches to others. His lectures are interspersed with powerful admonitions to the wicked, and he handles Universalism with gloves of steel." [1]

The endurance of the man was certainly very remarkable. After his visit to Portland, he returned to his home in Low Hampton, having been absent from there nearly six months, and having delivered three hundred and twenty-seven lectures.

The following May found him in New York City lecturing at the corner of Norfolk and Broom Streets from the 16th to the 29th. Later on he wrote to his sons:

"I have more business on hand than any two men like me should perform. I must lecture twice a day. I must converse with many — answer a host of questions — write answers to letters from all parts of the compass — from Canada to Florida, from Maine to Missouri. I must read all the candid arguments (which I confess are not many) which are urged against me. I must read all the slang of the drunken and sober . . . the polar star must be kept in view; the chart consulted, the compass watched, the reckoning kept; the sails set, the ship cleared, the sailors fed; the voyage prosecuted; the port of rest to which we are destined, understood; and to the Watchman call, 'Watchman, what of the night?'"

Yet he loved to feel the press and stress of this situation which he himself had created. There was an exhilaration in hearing of a Baptist here and a Methodist there, and others forming the band of preachers that was now becoming an important factor in spreading the warning. And all the time his ability to influence his listeners increased, and his assurance was increasing, and he felt surer and surer of his facts.

[1] N.B. The Universalists had come out against eternal damnation.

The oftener he reiterated his warning that the end would come between 1843 and 1844, the more he believed it and the more his deluded followers believed it.

Elder Columbus Green wrote an account of the impression he made while giving a course of lectures in Colchester, Vermont, in August:

"The audiences were very large; notwithstanding it was a time of general excitement, our place of worship was as still as death. His lectures were delivered in a most kind and affectionate manner — convincing every mind that he believed the sentiments he uttered. He made the most powerful exhortations that I ever heard fall from the lips of any one. A deep solemnity pervaded the minds of the community. Young men and maidens amid the pleasures of early years; men in the meridian of life, hurrying on with locomotive speed in pursuit of the treasures of earth; grey-haired sires, and matrons whose hoary locks gave evidence that many winters had passed over them, all paused and pondered on the things they heard — inquiring, 'Am I ready?'" [1]

By this time the spreading of Miller's prophecy was making great headway and was being disseminated through the country by such large numbers of self-elected preachers that it was deemed wise to hold a convention, and Boston was decided upon as the meeting ground. Great preparations for it were under way when the unexpected happened; — Prophet Miller, the central figure upon whom the eyes of the public were gazing with a strange mixture of curiosity, antagonism, fear, admiration, and credulity, fell ill with typhoid fever. It was a blow to his followers, but the one who suffered most

[1] Sylvester Bliss, *Life of William Miller.*

from the deprivation involved was himself. This stroke of destiny fell upon August 8, 1840. On the 15th he was able to dictate a few lines to be read at the Conference. The poor old man was well-nigh heartbroken.

"Oh, I had vainly hoped to see you all," he wrote, "to breathe and feel that sacred flame of love, of heavenly fire; to hear and speak of that dear blessed Saviour's near approach! ... But here I am, a weak, feeble, toil-worn old man upon a bed of sickness, with feeble nerves, and worse than all a heart, I fear, in part unreconciled to God. But, bless the Lord, O my soul! I have great blessings yet — more than I can number. I was not taken sick far from home; I am in the bosom of my family; — I have my reason; I can think, believe, and love. ... My hope is in Him who will soon come, and will not tarry. — I love the thought. It makes my bed in sickness; I hope it will in death. I wait for Him. — My soul, wait thou on God! ..."

How strange are the inconsistencies of the human mind! — Prophet Miller when preaching in health said one thing, but when ill he said another, and became like any other poor frail mortal and spoke of death with apparently the same sense of its inevitableness. In the grip of fever he seems to have momentarily forgotten that one of the most important tenets of his doctrine which he had been impressing upon the public mind was that he and all who believed as he did would never taste of death, but on some day or night, now swiftly approaching when the sound of the trumpet would ring throughout the Universe, would be caught up into the air, while the earth and the evildoers thereon would burn to ashes.

But it so happened that he recovered and was in the field again in December, weaker and more shaken, but as determined as ever to arouse the world to its impending doom.

In the mean time Elder Joshua V. Himes had had it all his own way. He sent preachers north, south, east, and west with charts and diagrams to demonstrate the correctness of Prophet Miller's calculations. He travelled here, there, and everywhere himself spreading the doctrine; — he printed and distributed pamphlets by the thousands, announcing the approach of the Day of Judgment; — he stirred up revivals and planned a campaign of camp-meetings for the opening of spring; — he left no stone unturned, so that now the atmosphere was charged with a high voltage of expectation that even scoffers were beginning to feel. The fact that in his preface to the Miller "Memoirs" he admits the responsibility of publishing and spreading abroad this doctrine places him in a position which the public felt justified in criticising: He says in this: "We hold the doctrine of a man's responsibility for the sentiments which he publishes, whether they are his own or another's. He is accountable to the community at the Great Tribunal for the good or bad they produce."

Such a statement as this leads to the assumption that he must have finally accepted the whole doctrine root and branch; otherwise his actions are unexplainable.

Trouble was looming up before them now in a number of ways which they had not foreseen. A spirit of aggressive opposition was showing itself. There were many who resented Miller's prophecy. In many cases a sort of superstitious fear was at the root of the resentment which led to acts of violence on the part of the city hoodlums, but the first real outbreak occurred in the quiet town of Newburyport. Essex County has always had its own unequivocal methods of showing disapproval, as history can tell, and this time was no exception to the rule.

Prophet Miller had promised to deliver his course of lectures there, and a great crowd gathered to hear them. At the first one, just as he was starting to speak, an egg was flung at him. Fortunately, it did not hit him, but fell on the desk close to his elbow. It was an ominous warning of what was to come, but he stood his ground and continued his lecture. Outside a mob was gathering in the street, and the noise of scuffling feet and the hum of excited voices could be distinctly heard, causing great concern to those inside. Just as the lecture was drawing to a close, an avalanche of stones came whizzing through the windows. The sound of smashing glass and the appearance of these dangerous missiles caused a panic in the audience. Men and women pushed and elbowed each other in a frantic attempt to leave the hall while more stones came scattering in among them. Soon the place was empty, and Miller also had to make a hasty retreat. But the doughty old Prophet was not to be discouraged by such demonstrations, nor was he to be prevented from delivering his lectures. The next evening saw him facing an even larger audience than the first one, only this time it was in the chapel in Hale's Court where they were safe from a repetition of the disturbance.

It was a great strain on him to meet the controversies and the criticism now awakened by his lectures. The newspapers were full of letters from protesting patrons, demanding answers to innumerable questions, which he could not ignore. One anonymous letter especially touched him on a sore point, and he read it out to his audience at one of his lectures.

"Mr. Miller," it read, "how dare you assert your theory with so much confidence without a knowledge of the Hebrew or Greek languages?"

The writer followed up this question with one or two Biblical quotations, the wording of which was not absolutely correct, which gave Prophet Miller an opportunity to make one of his ready retorts with true Yankee tartness.

"If I am not acquainted with Hebrew and Greek, I know enough to quote the English texts of the Scriptures rightly," was his reply, much to the approbation of his audience.

But to meet the arguments of the clergy of various denominations required a vast amount of thought and assurance, and besides his lectures he wrote a number of books replying to their criticisms, published by Elder Joshua V. Himes, and this made inroads upon his powers of physical endurance, especially as he was suffering from painful abscesses upon his leg which spread to the other leg, making locomotion difficult in the extreme. In this direful condition, and upon hearing of the death of his mother, he wrote to Elder Himes on December 7, 1842, as follows:

". . . The fatigue of body and mind has almost unnerved this old frame, and unfitted me to endure the burdens which Providence calls upon me to bear. I find as I grow old I grow more peevish and cannot bear so much contradiction, therefor I am called uncharitable and severe. No matter — this frail life will soon be over. My Master will soon call me home, and soon the scoffer and I shall be in another world to render our account before a righteous tribunal. I will therefore appeal to the Supreme Court of the Universe for the redress of grievances, and the rendering of judgment in my favor, by a revocation of the judgment of the Court below.

"The World and Clergy *vs.* Miller —

"I remain looking for the blessed hope.

"WM. MILLER."

He was pretty well tired out — the poor old Prophet!

But now the great year — the year of all years was about to dawn — the year in which his prophecy was to come true — according to his belief — *1843!* — the point of time toward which thousands were now turning — some in curiosity — some in scorn; but others with glowing hearts and beating pulses, making ready to watch for the coming of the Lord, stood looking for further signs in the heavens, and for the signs of the times — for distress of nations and for famine and pestilence; some ran hither and thither; and there were rumors, and rumors upon rumors, and strange sights, and strange sounds; — even the scoffers grew uneasy!

As the agitation and nervousness spread, Elder Joshua V. Himes, ever ready, published and distributed broadcast a pamphlet, called "Letter to Everybody," on the cover of which were the following terrifying words of warning:

"My friend! — the Day of the Lord is at hand! — and when it cometh you and I shall pass into another state of being — a being of eternal glory or eternal torment! *Believe it! believe it!* It cometh suddenly, in an instant of time, all things continuing as they were up to the very instant of the bursting in of the Lord upon the world. You are gazing along the sky — you see a lightning light along it — *it is the Lord!* You are speaking to your wife or your child by your fireside — an awful thunder breaks upon you — *it is the Lord!* You are sleeping in your bed — you hear a fearful crash — *it is the Lord!* You are awake in an hour of midnight darkness — you behold a fearful stream of brightness blaze in upon you — *it is the Lord!* You are riding in the cars, or upon your horse, or buying in the market, or working in the field, or busied in your garden, or looking over your accounts, or getting bread for your family, or eating it with them, or reading a book — you feel the earth tremble with a fearful shaking under your feet — *it is the Lord!* You go to the door to meet a mother, a brother, or a friend — *you meet the Lord!* Awful day! Awful coming! — 'Prepare to meet your God!' Prepare to meet His day! Prepare to meet His judgment! Prepare! Prepare!"

Thus entered the crucial year of *1843!*

### "THE ALARM"

"We are living, we are dwelling
    In a grand and awful time;
In an age on ages telling
    To be living is sublime.

"Hark the waking up of nations,
    Gog and Magog to the fray;
Hark! what soundeth? Is Creation
    Groaning for its latter day?

"Hark the onset! Will you fold your
    Faith-clad arms in lazy lock?
Up, O, up! thou drowsy soldier —
    Worlds are charging to the shock!" [1]

[1] *The Millennial Harp.* Published by Joshua V. Himes, 1843.

## CHAPTER V

### THE GREAT COMET

> "A pathless Comet, —
> The menace of the Universe;
> Still rolling on with innate force,
> Without a sphere, without a course."

THE year had no sooner opened than fanaticism, which had been held more or less in abeyance, now broke loose. Before this, the impending cataclysm seemed far away, but now the days were slipping by and the nerves of those who had accepted Prophet Miller's calculations began to feel on edge. Even the unbelievers and the scoffers insensibly felt the influence of the constant reiterations of the fact that the end of all things was at hand. The newspapers were full of it. The public talked of it, and discussed the possibilities of it in lecture halls; on the street corners; in all places where groups of people met together. The orthodox clergy were filled with dismay at finding a nervous dread percolating through their congregations. Wherever Prophet Miller and his co-workers held meetings, the crowds gathered, and among them were many who belonged to denominations strongly opposed to the approaching Second Advent doctrine, as interpreted by Prophet Miller. In a frantic effort to stem the tide of delusion the Bishop of Vermont, the Reverend John Henry Hopkins, D.D., wrote as follows, in an article which was published in pamphlet form and given a wide circulation:

"Full of presumption and of peril do we consider the at-

THE MILES FARM AT LEOMINSTER, MASSACHUSETTS

Glorious Millerite meetings were held in the barn in 1843 and 1844.

tempt to fix the day or the year of our Lord's coming. Full of presumption because Christ himself declares, 'of that day and hour knoweth no man, no, not the angels of God, but my Father only.' And again, 'It is not for you to know the times and the seasons which the Father hath put in His own power.' Full of presumption because one man sets himself above the thousands upon thousands of all the teachers, preachers, confessors, and martyrs that have gone before him. Full of presumption because St. Peter declares 'that no prophecy is of any private interpretation' (St. Peter, 1st–26th), and yet it is nothing but private interpretation that is offered us; and although it be, indeed, with as much confidence as if it were sanctioned by the consent of the whole Church of God.

"The scheme under consideration claims for its author a man of strong mind and much native talent. And we freely acknowledge that his lectures and chart display uncommon ingenuity and great familiarity with the Scriptures. It appears to have been the main object of his studies for several years of his life to master the difficulties of unfulfilled prophecy, and the result, whether he be right or wrong, is at least a very remarkable proof of persevering concentration of thought, and has secured for him thus far an extraordinary measure of public attention and notoriety. . . . Many, very many visionary enthusiasts have undertaken to warn mankind of the approaching judgment — and never yet have they failed in obtaining a numerous auditory and a willing ear. Powerful excitement, extravagant wildness, the intoxication of fanaticism, the ravings of madness, have all followed in their train. And yet, alas! these were called the fruits of the study of prophecy — as if the Word of God, in the strongest and clearest terms, had not pronounced against the possibility of our foreknowing the time of our Lord's appearing; as if in the very last chapter of Holy Scripture the Almighty had not pronounced wrath upon the 'adding to the word of prophecy' — a sin which we fear is but too often unwittingly committed by the presumptuous inferences of human calculation.

"Contemplating, therefore, the history of the past, no intelligent or instructed mind can wonder at the success, as it is unhappily considered, of the present delusion. And since it has been unfortunately chosen by the Author that a whole year shall be assigned for the fulfilment of his prediction, instead of contenting himself with a day, like most of his predecessors, we should naturally be led to anticipate that the excitement would increase as the time announced draws near to its termination — so that if already so many deplorable examples of extravagance have occurred, it is hard to imagine the awful extent to which they may be carried when the last week of the allotted period begins to run. In this respect the scheme under consideration is more mischievous than any which has yet been inflicted on the community, for it keeps the intense fever of fanaticism burning for more than a year, whereas in the other cases a single day brought the disorder to its crisis, and therefore the patients were more likely to recover." [1]

The Reverend Abel C. Thomas was another clergyman who strove to educate the public. He was a Universalist, and was settled in Lowell as pastor of the Second Church in 1843,

[1] Published in 1843.

having had a call there from Philadelphia. He was a learned man whose opinion was valued.

"The phrase 'the end of the world,'" he wrote, "occurs seven times in the New Testament. The Greek term rendered world is not *kosmos* (which signifies the *material* world), but *aion*, which signifies *era* or *age*. Its meaning is well expressed when we speak of the Christian era, the Jewish era, the Elizabethan era — or Golden Age — the Dark Ages, and the like. The Disciples asked our Lord in a private interview, 'What shall be the sign of thy coming, and of the end of the world?' (aion.) In the reply of our Saviour he speaks thrice of the *end* — namely, *the end of the world* inquired for, and He assures His Disciples that the end would be before that generation had passed away. . . .

". . . There is not a place in Scripture where the end of *kosmos* is mentioned, but the end of *aion* is seven times spoken of in the New Testament. 'The Harvest is the end of the world' (aion). Matt. XIII — verse 48. 'So shall it be at the end of the world' (aion)." [1]

It made little difference, however, to the followers of Prophet Miller that the opposing clergy refuted his theory. They were under the spell of a delusion that was stronger than any argument denouncing it. They pointed to Daniel's vision and to King Nebuchadnezzar's dream, and to their prophet's interpretation of the ram, the he-goat, and exceeding Great Horn, and the fulfilment of the prophecy. To this a counter-statement was made, declaring that the eighth chapter of Daniel, which contained the crux of Mil-

---

[1] *A Complete Refutation of Miller's Theory of the End of the World in 1843.* Published in 1843. See Appendix, pp. 263–64.

ler's theory according to his personal interpretation of it, had nothing to do with the coming of Christ, or the setting up of God's everlasting Kingdom. Antiochus Epiphanes, a Syrian king, they claimed, was the central figure in the Prophet Daniel's vision. The twenty-three hundred days spoken of therein were to be interpreted as half-days, amounting to eleven hundred and fifty literal days, which were literally fulfilled by Antiochus and his persecution of the Jews and the desecration of the Temple, about one hundred and sixty years before Christ.[1] But this failed to impress the excited brains of those who were watching for the Great Day — they believed in William Miller and his theory, and no amount of lucid explanation from orthodox churches produced any effect upon them.

The following account of a scene that occurred in Washington, written by a correspondent of the "Boston Mercantile Journal" to the editor, will show how, in spite of the efforts of the orthodox clergy to explain what they considered to be the weak points of his arguments, the public, or a certain portion of it, were hysterically eager to hear from Miller's own lips his reasons for believing that the Day of Judgment was at hand:

WASHINGTON, *Jan. 22d*, 1843.

"MR. SLEEPER:

"I wrote you yesterday among other news that Mr. Miller, the *end-of-the-world man, was here.* It was announced yesterday, by hand-bills stuck up all over the city, that he would preach to-day (Sunday) at three o'clock P.M. from the steps of the Patent Office; and immediately after dinner,

[1] *Our First Century.* Published in 1881.

crowds were observed wending their way in that direction. The Commissioner of the Public Buildings, or some other officer, had had erected a barricade about halfway up the steps, for the purpose of keeping off the crowd; and when I went to the place of meeting, the space between Seventh and Ninth Streets, in front of the Patent Office, was nearly filled with people, their numbers variously estimated from five to ten thousand, of all sexes, ages, and colors. I should think there were over five thousand.

"The space above the barricades was guarded by police officers, who had permitted some few persons, principally members of Congress, to pass over, which filled some of the unfavored ones with no little indignation, and the democratic spirit of the people began to work.

"A number of abortive attempts were made to pass the barrier, but, except for the privileged few, unsuccessfully. One person, however, more determined than the rest, showed fight, and was roughly handled by the officers, when the crowd, taking his part and presuming he was abused, made a rush to the barrier to break it down, but for the moment unsuccessfully. The crowd became, however, more calm until a gentleman, whom I understood to be a clergyman, stepped forward and said that he had been requested to inform the people before him 'that there was no certain information that Mr. Miller was in the city'; upon which a shout arose unlike anything I have heard since the shouts on Bunker Hill in September, 1840 — intermingled with cries of 'Hoax!' 'Humbug!' etc.

"The crowd, however, became still enough in a few minutes for the clergyman to continue his remarks which were as follows: 'As I said before, Mr. Miller is probably not in the city; but as it is a pity that such a concourse should be entirely disappointed of receiving benefit on such a day, I think it would be well for you to call on a distinguished gentleman, Mr. Briggs, a member of Congress from Massachusetts, to give you a temperance address. He is now on the platform.'

"Cries of 'Briggs!' 'Briggs!' ensued; but Mr. Briggs had no notion of being called on in this unceremonious manner, and, though urgently solicited by his friends, declined. The crowd, perceiving there was to be no 'fun' made for them, determined to make some for themselves; and again rushing against the barricade, this time successfully, succeeded in obtaining a footing on the platform, and drove the privileged ones, *ladies and all*, through the Patent Office — the door of which was kicked open — into the basement, and from thence into the street; and then, as far as I know, quietly dispersed."

It was thought by many that mischievous persons had printed and distributed the hand-bills in order to fool the public, but no authentic explanation was ever forthcoming.

Mr. Miller's biographer gives an account of the actions of a vast audience that crowded the large hall of the Chinese Museum in Philadelphia to hear the Prophet speak in February. He lectured from the 3d to the 10th. Every evening the people flocked to the lectures, but one evening, the evening of the 7th, he had a very agitating experience. The crowd had begun to arrive very early, and the hall was filled to its utmost capacity.

"When the lecture commenced," Elder Bliss asserts, "the

crowd and confusion were so great as to render it almost impossible to hear the speaker; and it was thought best, after notifying the people what was to be done and giving an opportunity for all who wished to do so to go out — to close the doors and thus secure silence. This was done, and the speaker proceeded to his subject. For about half an hour there was profound silence, and deep interest was evinced by the immense audience, with the exception of a few unruly boys. This would have undoubtedly continued, had it not been for the circumstance of a lady fainting, and it becoming necessary to open the doors for her to go out. When the door was opened, there was a rush of persons who stood outside for admittance. As soon as this was done, and a few had come into the room, an unruly boy raised the cry of 'Fire!' which threw the whole assembly into confusion, some crying one thing, and some another. There did not appear to be any disposition on the part of the multitude to disturb the meeting; but all came from the rush and the cry. The disorder arose more from the excited fears of the people than from any other cause.

"Order was again restored, and the speaker proceeded for a few moments when another rush was made, and the excitement became so great within as to render it expedient to dismiss the meeting. The police of the city were willing to do what they could, but there was nothing for them to do; for they could not govern the excited nerves of the audience."

A few evenings later, the multitude again assembled, and excitement again prevailed so that the owners of the hall became alarmed and ordered the meetings to be discontinued.

When Prophet Miller announced this fact, it was unexpected, and the audience was moved beyond expression. "Probably more than a thousand persons arose to testify their faith in the truth of the near Advent," Elder Bliss continues, "and three or four hundred of the unconverted arose to request an interest in his prayers. Mr. Miller closed the service by a most feeling and appropriate prayer and the benediction."

In contrast to the days when, unmolested, he could preach his doctrine throughout the rural districts, Miller now suddenly found himself attacked on all sides — many even declaring him to be insane. The editor of the "Gazette and Advertiser" of Long Island commented thus upon this last statement, after having interviewed him in February, 1843:

"Our curiosity was recently gratified by an introduction to this gentleman, who has probably been an object of more abuse, ridicule, and blackguardism than any other man now living. A large number of the veracious editors of the political and religious newspapers have assured us that Mr. Miller was totally insane, and sundry preachers have confirmed this assurance. We were somewhat surprised to hear him converse with a coolness and soundness of judgment which made us whisper to ourselves: 'If this be madness, then there is method in it.'"

A great many articles, written for the purpose of refuting his doctrine, were answered by Miller, but, if this was a tax on his strength, it was as nothing to what was now proving to be a distinct menace to his cause, namely, the uncanny influence which was being exerted over great numbers of persons of all ages by a Congregational minister, the Reverend

John Starkweather by name, who had graduated from the Theological Seminary at Andover and who had now ostensibly become one of his followers. At one time this gentleman had been pastor of the Marlborough Chapel in Boston, and while occupying that pulpit had acquired a reputation of very extreme sanctity, so much so that when Elder Himes left his own pulpit to travel all over the country to warn people that the end of the world was near at hand, he chose him as one eminently fitted to take charge of his congregation at the Chardon Street Chapel during his absence.

Now the Reverend John Starkweather was noted among his parishioners as a handsome man. He had a fine figure and prepossessing manners, and a voice that exerted a most extraordinary influence over those who listened to it. No one could explain what constituted the charm of it, or the compelling power in it, but he had hardly started preaching before the chapel was crowded to its doors. It very soon became evident that he held strange and exceedingly peculiar beliefs of his own which had not been put forth before, and these he proceeded to instill into the already agitated minds of Elder Himes's flock. The one he laid the greatest stress upon was that real conversion must not only be of the spirit, but must be manifested in the body as well, and before any one realized what the effect of such a doctrine would be, hundreds who listened to him began to fall into cataleptic trances, and others were seized with epileptic fits and rolled upon the ground writhing as though in agony, while still others lost all their strength and sank in heaps, apparently too feeble to sit upright. When demonstrations of this sort happened, he declared them to be signs of the power of God cleansing their souls of sin. He called it the "sealing power," and those who did not experience it immediately sought vigorously to attain it — usually succeeding so well as to strike terror and awe in those who were not yet wholly prepared to accept this dangerous theory.

By the time Elder Himes returned from his travels, he found his congregation in the throes of the wildest fanaticism, and the outside public in a ferment of indignation and disgust. History has proved that Prophet Miller and Elder Himes as well, were past-masters at stirring a congregation or the crowds in a lecture hall up to a high pitch of hysterical excitement, but neither of them was for a moment ready to countenance any such manifestations as were induced by the peculiar influence exerted by the Reverend John Starkweather.

At first they questioned whether he consciously exerted this power; but it did not take them long to find out that not only did he consciously exert it, but he did so wherever and whenever the opportunity presented itself. They realized also that such proceedings as were now taking place in the Chardon Street Chapel would place all of those connected with the Miller doctrine in disrepute, as the author of the proceedings openly called himself a follower of Prophet Miller. Elder Himes undertook to remonstrate with him, but to no avail. Finally things came to such a pass that something definite had to be done to warn those who were crowding to the meetings at the chapel that it was not a spiritual force that was throwing them into fits and contortions, but the mesmeric influence of the Reverend John Starkweather; — such influence being evil and to be shunned by every one who claimed to be a Christian. Accordingly he went to one of the meetings when as usual a crowd of deluded men and women and even children were thronging the doors, and he managed to make a public protest against what had been happening there during his absence. Mr. Starkweather immediately arose and became so vehement that, according to Elder Bliss, "Mr. Himes felt justified in again addressing the audience, and exposing the nature of the exercises that had appeared among them and their pernicious tendency."

"This," he goes on to say, "so shocked the sensibilities of those who regarded them as the great power of God that they cried out and stopped their ears. Some jumped up on their feet, and some ran out of the house. 'You will drive out the Holy Ghost!' cried one. 'You are throwing on cold water!' cried another. 'Throwing on cold water!' retorted Mr. Himes. 'I would throw on the Atlantic Ocean before I would be identified with such abominations as these, or suffer them in this place unrebuked!'"

A stormy scene ensued, the result of which was that the Reverend John Starkweather declared that he and "the saints," as he called those addicted to falling into fits, would no longer meet at the Marlborough Chapel, but would find a more congenial place elsewhere; whereupon he marched down the aisle and out of the door, followed by the congregation and leaving Elder Himes standing alone by the reading-desk.

From this time on the Reverend John Starkweather gathered about him a following wholly his own, but Prophet Miller had to bear the brunt of the criticism aroused by their immoderate behavior owing to the fact that the former gentleman was as insistent that the world was coming to an end as he was, therefore the public always supposed them to be true Millerites.

The following anecdote gives an idea of the direful effects of Mr. Starkweather's mesmeric influence on the mentality of his admirers:

"As a specimen of the hallucination," Elder Bliss informs us, "on returning from a meeting a young man by the name of M—— imagined that he had power to hold the cars from moving on the railroad by the mere effort of his will. As they were about starting, he said, 'Don't you go!' The wheels of the locomotive made several revolutions before the heavy train started. 'Now, go!' he said — and it moved. 'There!' said he, 'did I not stop the train?'"

The question was addressed to his father, who was duly impressed, and on their way home the young man became ambitious to make another demonstration of the power of the Spirit.

"'Father,' said he, 'do you believe I have the power of God?'

"'Yes,' said the father, who had been fascinated at the meeting.

"'Well, then, *drive the horse on to that rock by the roadside!*' And he was obeyed — somewhat to their discomfort!"

At another meeting, held at Windsor, Connecticut, something equally senseless occurred of which Elder Collins gave an account that same year in the "Signs of the Times": "One female believed that as Peter walked on the sea by faith, so she, by faith, might walk across the Connecticut

River, and resolved to make the attempt, but was prevented."

As a result of this interference Elder Collins goes on to say: "They kept the meeting in confusion for an hour or two, and would listen to no remonstrances."

It was now forced upon Prophet Miller's mind that he was beginning to lose control of the situation. He had, indeed, "sown the wind," and from every quarter was coming the rumblings of the whirlwind.

In a state of hysterical enthusiasm the self-made preachers of his doctrine now let loose their own imaginings, and every town and village had its own version of the great prophecy. Moreover, he was besieged by requests from his impatient followers to name the day when the end was to come. The indefiniteness of his prophecy in giving it a year in which to fulfil itself made them restive.

About this time, according to Elder Bliss, the "New York Herald" announced through its columns that the Millerites had fixed upon April 3d as the day when the end would come, and this bit of news went the length and breadth of the land. This led Professor Moses Stuart, who had published a pamphlet refuting the theory upon which the prophecy was based, to refer to Miller and his followers as "the men of April 3d, 1843."

"I would suggest," he says in this pamphlet, "that in some way or other they have in all probability made a small mistake as to the exact day of the month when the great catastrophe takes place — the *1st of April* being evidently much more appropriate to the arrangements than any other day in the year." [1]

---

[1] *Hints*, 2d ed., p. 173.

To which the "New York Observer" of February 11, 1843, responds approvingly, declaring that Professor Stuart's suggestion was conducive to "*quieting every feeling of alarm!*"

The "Sandy Hill Herald," a paper published in Miller's own county, took up his cudgels to the extent of remonstrating with a certain amount of sympathy against such ridicule:

"We are not prepared to say how far the old man is from correct, but one thing, *we doubt not that he is sincere*. Certainly all who have heard him lecture, or have read his works, must acknowledge that he is a sound reasoner, and, as such, is entitled to fair arguments from those who differ with him. Yet his opponents do not see fit to exert their reasoning powers, but content themselves by denouncing the old gentleman as a 'fanatic,' a 'liar,' 'deluded old fool,' 'speculator,' etc. Mr. Miller is now, and has been for many years, a resident of this county, and as a citizen, a man, and a Christian, stands high in the estimation of all who know him; and we have been pained to hear the grey-headed, trembling old man denounced as a 'speculating knave!'"

The Pittsburgh, Pennsylvania, "Gazette" took up more or less the same vein, and in one of its issues of that year made the following comments:

"We do not concur with Mr. Miller in his interpretations of the prophecies; but we see neither reason nor Christianity in the unmerited reproach which is heaped upon him for an honest opinion. And that he is honest we have no doubt. True, we think him in error, but we believe he is honestly so. ... The truth is, as far as we apprehend, that many of those who are so indecorous and vituperative in their denunciations of Miller are in fearful trepidation, lest the day being so near at hand 'should overtake them unawares,' and hence, like cowardly boys in the dark, they make a great noise by way of keeping up their courage, and to frighten away the bugbears."

One of the greatest trials to William Miller, however, was the evidence that came from every quarter that he no longer wholly controlled his followers. Brother Knapp (a most fiery man), Brother Litch, Brother Storrs, Brother Fitch, Brother Kirk, Brother Bliss, Brother Patten, Brother Beach, Brother Whitney, Brother Hook, Brother Galusha, and a host of others ostensibly preaching according to his doctrine, were, in reality, taking matters a good deal into their own hands and asserting their own ideas with apparent authority. He wrote the following words of warning to them:

"DEAR BRETHREN:

"This year, according to our faith, is the last year that Satan will reign in our earth. Jesus Christ will come, and bruise his head. The kingdom of the earth will be dashed to pieces, which is the same thing. . . . The world will watch for our halting. They cannot think we believe what we speak, for they count our faith a strange faith; and now, beware, and not give them any vantage-ground over us. They will perhaps look for the halting and falling away of many. But I hope none who are looking for the glorious appearing will let their faith waver. Keep cool, let patience have its perfect work. . . . This year will try our faith; we must be tried, purified, and made white; and if there should be any amongst us who do not in heart believe, they will go out from us; — but I am persuaded that there cannot be many such. . . . I beseech you, my dear brethren, be careful that Satan get no advantage over you by scattering coals of wild-fire among you; for, if he cannot drive you into unbelief and doubt, he will try his wild-fire of fanaticism and speculation to get us from the Word of God. Be watchful and sober, and hope to the end. . . . Let us then stand strong in the faith, with our loins girt about with truth, and our lamps trimmed and burning and waiting for our Lord — ready to enter the promised land, the true inheritance of the saints. This year the fulness of time will come; the shout of victory will be heard in heaven; the triumphant return of our Great Captain may be expected, the new song will commence before the throne, eternity begin its revolution, and time shall be no more.

"This year — O glorious year! — the trump of Jubilee will be blown, the exiled children will return, the pilgrims reach their home, from earth and heaven the scattered remnants come and meet in middle air — the fathers before the flood, Noah and his sons — Abraham and his, the Jew and Gentile. . . . This year! the long-looked-for year of years! the best! — it has come!"

But the warning to "keep cool" fell upon deaf ears — it had come too late. Already the wild-fire spoken of was leaping from heart to heart and from brain to brain throughout the entire host of credulous human beings now under the spell of Miller's prophecy. It made no difference that no specific day had been set by him during that fateful year; his followers took counsel together and fixed on days according

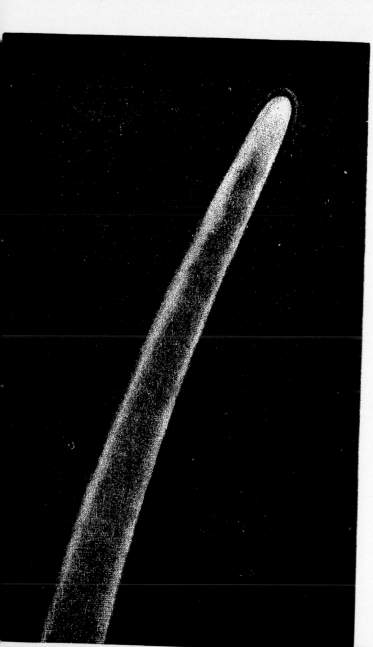

THE GREAT COMET OF 1843

"The absolute diameter of the nebulosity surrounding the head was about thirty-six thousand miles. The length of the tail was prodigious. At its greatest visible length it was one hundred and eight millions of miles long."

to their liking — some inclining toward the dates of the Passover and the Crucifixion, while others looked forward to the season of the Ascension, or the Feast of the Pentecost, as the most probable time for the Lord to come. In the villages and hamlets — in the towns and cities — men and women gazed upward with eager eyes — waiting for the signs of what was to come.

The tension and nervous exhaustion were too great for Prophet Miller. While lecturing in the vicinity of Saratoga Springs, he was seized with an attack of what was supposed to be erysipelas in his right arm, and his son was hastily sent for to take him to his home in Low Hampton. On April 6th he wrote as follows to Elder Himes: "I am now at home; was brought home six days since. I am very weak in body, but, blessed be God! my mind, faith, and hope are yet strong in the Lord — no wavering in my belief that I shall see Christ this year. . . ."

He was unable to finish his letter, but his son forwarded it just as it was to Elder Himes — writing a few lines himself in which he said: "Father is quite low and feeble, and we fear he may be no better."

According to his biographer, Elder Bliss, "His complaint manifested itself in a multiplicity and succession of car-buncle boils, which were a great drain on his system and wasted his strength rapidly."

On May 3, 1843, he made another attempt to write to Elder Himes:

"My health is on the gain as my folks would say," he wrote. "I have now *only* twenty-two boils, from the bigness of a grape to a walnut, on my shoulder, sides, back, and arms! I am truly afflicted like Job and have about as many comforters, only they do not come to see me as Job's did."

After this as there was no improvement, his son notified Elder Himes as follows: "Father's health is no better on the whole. He continues very weak and low, confined to his bed most of the time."

The fever which now took hold of him in addition to his other trouble proved almost too much for Prophet Miller. He came very near to leaving the earth before the allotted time left for its existence was half exhausted.

Blank consternation marked the faces of his followers. Elder Himes and Brother Storrs, Brother Litch, Brother Fitch, and all the brotherhood of preachers and lecturers, stood in the breach and exhorted them with ringing voices to stand firm in the faith.

It was a critical moment. Then without warning something unexpected happened that turned the tide and swept it onward toward its flood. At noonday, when the sun shone brightly, a great rival light appeared in the sky blazing out against the blue! People ran out of their houses to look at it; pedestrians stood in the streets gazing upward in amazement; news of it spread like lightning, and in the cities and towns, and along the highways and byways leading to distant villages and secluded hamlets, groups of excited men and women and frightened children stood staring at the celestial stranger.

It was a comet! — the great resplendent *comet of 1843!* — famous in history as one of the greatest ever seen to approach our sphere.

Its appearance created a sensation everywhere, but the

exaltation of Miller's followers knew no bounds. Here, indeed, was a sign to justify their confidence in the near approach of the end of all things terrestrial! Breathlessly they hastened to and fro "sounding an alarm to be on the watch for what was now evidently nigh unto the doors."

There are various accounts to be found of the great comet of 1843. The following is taken from "Our First Century," published by C. A. Nichols & Co., in 1881:

### "SUDDEN APPEARANCE OF A GREAT AND FIERY COMET IN THE SKIES AT NOONDAY, 1843.

"The Comet of 1843 is regarded as perhaps the most marvellous of the present age, having been observed in the daytime even before it was visible at night — passing very near the sun, exhibiting an enormous length of tail; and arousing interest in the public mind as universal and deep as it was unprecedented. It startled the world by its sudden apparition in the spring in the western heavens, like a streak of aurora streaming from the region of the sun, below the Constellation of Orion. It was at first mistaken by multitudes for the zodiacal light, but its aspect and movements soon proved it to be a comet of the largest class. There were, too, some persons who, without regarding it like many of the then numerous sect called Millerites, as foretokening the speedy destruction of the world, still could not gaze at it untroubled by a certain nameless feeling of doubt and fear. . . . When its distance from the sun allowed it to be visible after sunset, it presented an appearance of extraordinary magnificence."

The sight of the awe-inspiring and mysterious visitor

brought to the minds of many apprehensive persons a description of the Last Day which appeared in a book called "A View of the Expected Christian Millennium," by Joshua Priest, published in 1828, but which was being read with especial interest at this time. One extract will be sufficient to show how it served to intensify the uneasiness caused by the appearance of this wanderer of the Universe:

"For lo! the planets will begin to wander from their orbs, and dash one against the other; for now is lost the latent principle of the centrifugal power which operates on all the planets, and inclines them to fly off in straight lines into interminable space, which necessarily will give them a tremendous centripetal force toward the sun. That body being the centre, or lowest point in the system, is therefore the centre of attraction to all the planets.

"Here, then, in their descent toward the sun will be a horrible realization of the stars falling from heaven, and of the power of the heavens being shaken; and long before they reach the sun, will dash one against the other, and will be a wreck of matter and a crush of worlds on fire!"

> "The great Archangel's trump shall sound
> (While twice ten thousand thunders roar),
> Tear up the graves, and cleave the ground,
> And make the greedy sea restore.
>
> "The greedy sea shall yield her dead,
> The earth no more her slain conceal;
> Sinners shall lift their guilty heads,
> And shrink to see a yawning hell.
>
> "We, while the stars from heaven shall fall,
> And mountains are on mountains hurled,
> Shall stand unmoved amidst them all,
> And smile to see a burning world.

VIEW OF THE GREAT COMET OF 1843 WHEN NEAREST THE EARTH

"The earth and all the works therein
Dissolve, by raging flames destroyed;
While we survey the awful scene
And mount above the fiery void." [1]

[1] From *The Millennial Harp,* the hymn-book of the Millerites. Published
by Joshua V. Himes, 1843.

# CHAPTER VI

## CAMP–MEETINGS

"I am bound for the kingdom,
Will you go to glory with me?
Hallelujah, O Hallelujah!
I'm bound for the kingdom,
Will you go to glory with me?
Hallelujah, O praise the Lord!"

*Old camp-meeting hymn*, 1843

Now, when the spring opened, the camp-meetings began. A general feeling had prevailed for some time that the end would come in April, and, though there is no proof of any fixed date in that month having been given out by Prophet Miller, there is no doubt whatever that among his following many preached that the Great Day would come before the first of May. As soon as the weather permitted, therefore, the great Tabernacle tent was pitched, first in one place and then another, and the stir and excitement of the exhortations and the praying and singing drew crowds of frightened human beings as well as a host who went from curiosity to the Millerite Camp-Grounds. To one of these meetings went our New England poet, John Greenleaf Whittier, who wrote afterwards an interesting account of his impressions. Some of them are as follows, written in such descriptive language as to bring the scene vividly before the reader's eyes. We will follow the country road with him and hear him tell of what he saw:

"'Stage ready, gentlemen! Stage for camp-ground, Derry! Second Advent camp-meeting!'

"Accustomed as I begin to feel to the ordinary sights and sounds of this busy city, I was, I confess, somewhat startled by this business-like annunciation from the driver of a stage, who stood beside his horses swinging his whip with some degree of impatience: 'Seventy-five cents to the Second Advent camp-ground!' The stage was soon filled; the driver cracked his whip and went rattling down the street.

"The Second Advent — the coming of our Lord in person upon this earth, with signs, and wonders, and terrible judgments — the heavens rolling together as a scroll, the elements melting with fervent heat! The mighty consummation of all things at hand, with its destruction and its triumphs, sad wailings of the lost and rejoicing songs of the glorified! From this over-swarming hive of industry — from these crowded treadmills of gain — here were men and women going out in solemn earnestness to prepare for the dread moment which they verily suppose is only a few months distant — to lift up their warning voices in the midst of scoffers and doubters, and to cry aloud to blind priests and careless churches, 'Behold, the Bridegroom cometh!'

"It was one of the most lovely mornings of this loveliest season of the year; a warm, soft atmosphere; clear sunshine falling on the city's spires and roofs; the hills of Dracut quiet and green in the distance, with their white farm-houses and scattered trees; around me the continual tread of footsteps hurrying to the toils of the day; merchants spreading out their wares for the eyes of purchasers; sounds of hammers, the sharp clink of trowels, the murmur of the great manufactories subdued by distance. How was it possible, in the midst of so much life, in that sunrise light, and in view of all-abounding beauty, that the idea of the death of Nature — the baptism of the world in fire — could take such a practical shape as this? Yet here were sober, intelligent men, gentle and pious women, who, verily believing the end to be close at hand, had left their counting-rooms, and work-shops, and household cares to publish the great tidings, and to startle, if possible, a careless and unbelieving generation into preparation for the day of the Lord and for that blessed millennium — the restored paradise — when, renovated and renewed by its fire-purgation, the earth shall become as of old the garden of the Lord, and the saints alone shall inherit it. . . .

"I do not, I confess, sympathize with my Second Advent friends in the lamentable depreciation of Mother Earth even in her present state. I find it extremely difficult to comprehend how it is that this goodly, green, sunlit home of ours is resting under a curse. It really does not seem to me to be altogether like the roll which the angel bore in the prophet's vision, 'written within and without with mourning, lamentation, and woe.' September sunsets, changing forests, moonrise and cloud, sun and rain — I for one am contented with them. They fill my heart with a sense of beauty. I see in them the perfect work of infinite love as well as wisdom.

"It may be that our Advent friends, however, coincide with the opinion of an old writer on the prophecies, who considered the hills and valleys of the earth's surface and its changes of seasons as so many visible manifestations of God's curse, and that in the millennium, as in the days of Adam's innocence, all these picturesque inequalities would be levelled nicely away, and the flat surface laid handsomely down to grass!

"As might be expected, the effect of this belief in the speedy destruction of the world and the personal coming of the Messiah, acting upon a class of uncultivated, and in some cases gross minds, is not always in keeping with the enlightened Christian's ideal of the better day. One is shocked in reading some of the 'hymns' of these believers. Sensual images — semi-Mahometan descriptions of the condition of the 'saints' — exultations over the destruction of the 'sinners' — mingle with the beautiful and soothing promises of the prophets. There are, indeed, occasionally to be found among the believers men of refined and exalted spiritualism, who in their lives and conversation remind one of Tennyson's Christian knight-errant in his yearnings toward the hope set before him:

> "'To me is given
> Such hope I may not fear;
> I long to breathe the airs of heaven,
> Which sometimes meet me here.
>
> "'I muse on joys that cannot cease,
> Pure spaces filled with living beams,
> White lilies of eternal peace
> Whose odors haunt my dreams.'

"One of the most ludicrous examples of the sensual phase of Millerism, the incongruous blending of the sublime with the ridiculous, was mentioned to me not long since. A fashionable young woman in the western part of this State became an enthusiastic believer in the doctrine. On the day which had been designated as the closing one of time, she packed all her fine dresses and toilet valuables in a large trunk with long straps attached to it, and, seating herself upon it, buckled the straps over her shoulders, patiently awaiting the crisis — shrewdly calculating that, as she must herself go upwards, her goods and chattels would of necessity follow!"

Here the poet tells of a visit he made during the previous autumn to a camp-meeting in East Kingston.

"The spot was well chosen," he says. "A tall growth of pine and hemlock threw its melancholy shadow over the multitude, who were arranged upon rough seats of boards and logs. Several hundred — perhaps a thousand people — were present, and more were rapidly coming. Drawn about in a circle, forming a background of snowy whiteness to the dark masses of men and foliage, were the white tents, and back of them the provision-stalls and cook-shops. When I reached the ground, a hymn, the words of which I could not distinguish, was pealing through the dim aisles of the forest. I could readily perceive that it had its effect upon the multitude before me, kindling to higher intensity their already excited enthusiasm. The preachers were placed in a rude pulpit of rough boards, carpeted only by the dead forest leaves and flowers, and tasselled, not with silk and velvet, but with the green boughs of the sombre hemlocks around it. One of them followed the music in an earnest exhortation on the duty of preparing for the great event. Occasionally he was really eloquent, and his description of the last day had the ghastly distinctness of Anelli's painting of the End of the World.

"Suspended from the front of the rude pulpit were two broad sheets of canvas, upon one of which was the figure of a

THE GREAT MILLERITE CHART

Four by six feet in size. Painted on white linen.

man, the head of gold, the breast and arms of silver, the
belly of brass, the legs of iron, and the feet of clay — the
dream of Nebuchadnezzar. On the other were depicted the
wonders of the Apocalyptic vision — the beasts, the
dragons, the scarlet woman seen by the seer of Patmos,
Oriental types, figures, and mystic symbols, translated into
staring Yankee realities, and exhibited like the beasts of a
travelling menagerie. One horrible image, with its hideous
heads and scaly caudal extremity, reminded me of the
tremendous line of Milton, who, in speaking of the same evil
dragon, describes him as

"'Swindging the scaly horrors of his folded tail.'

"To an imaginative mind the scene was full of novel
interest. The white circle of tents; the dim wood arches; the
upturned, earnest faces; the loud voices of the speakers,
burdened with the awful symbolic language of the Bible; the
smoke from the fires, rising like incense — carried me back
to those days of primitive worship which tradition faintly
whispers of, when on hilltops, and in the shade of old woods,
Religion had her first altars, with every man for her priest,
and the whole universe for her temple.

"Wisely and truthfully has Dr. Channing spoken of this
doctrine of the Second Advent in his memorable discourse in
Berkshire a little before his death:

"'There are some among us at the present moment who
are waiting for the speedy coming of Christ. They expect,
before another year closes, . . . to hear His voice, to stand
before His judgment seat. These illusions spring from
misinterpretation of Scripture language. . . The Christian,

whose inward eyes and ears are touched by God, discerns
the coming of Christ, hears the sound of His chariot wheels
and the voice of His trumpet, when no other perceives them.
He discerns the Saviour's advent in the dawning of higher
truth on the world. . . . Christ comes in the conversion, the
regeneration, the emancipation, of the world.'" [1]

This visit of Whittier's to the camp-meeting at East
Kingston was in 1842, when a great solemnity prevailed and
held back much of the manifestations of hysteria which
came later. The late Daniel M. Treadwell describes a visit
to a camp-meeting that same year, in a book called "Reminiscences of Men and Things on Long Island," published in
1917. It must be said that he had little patience with
Miller's doctrine, but the earnestness of his followers evidently impressed him. The contents of the book are taken
from his journals which he started early in life, therefore he
did not have to rely upon his memory.

"*Sunday, August* 14, 1842. Went this day to see the great
Millerite encampment in Petit's woods, about one mile
south from the village of Hempstead. We believe they have
been encamped here about a week. This piece of primeval
woods is charmingly adapted and is held for purposes of this
kind. The grounds are fenced, or stockaded, and can be
closed at night against intruders. The encampment does
not in any essential differ from an ordinary Methodist
camp-meeting. There is a large shelter, or stand erected from
which sermons are preached or lectures delivered.

[1] John Greenleaf Whittier, *Prose Works*. Published, 1866, Ticknor &
Fields, Boston.

"There were seats erected sufficient to accommodate two thousand people; besides, there is a large tent capable of holding a great many people to be used in the emergency of bad weather. The private tents, of which there were a great many, were arranged about the grounds much as the ordinary camp-meeting. . . .

"There was a vast number of people on the grounds to-day, the greater portion of whom were attracted there out of curiosity, and the novelty of the occasion. . . .

"While the great crowd on the camp-ground who were not worshippers nor neophytes maintained a marvellous decorum, it was quite the reverse on the outside of the grounds; for a fourth of a mile north and south of the main entrance every conceivable traffic in bibulous fluids was carried on, and noisy vagabond crowds occupied booths on the highway. There was a constant stream of pedestrians going and coming from the village of Hempstead.

"The most attractive speaker during the day was Joshua V. Himes, chief saint and prophet. He spoke twice during the day from the outside stand. One Amasa Baker held forth from within the big tent. He was a fire-eater. He enunciated emphatically that all the saints who accepted the teachings of the prophet, and were prepared, would enter with Christ the kingdom in April next; — all others would be burned to a cinder by an avenging God. Many others preached, but the principal method for proselytizing was through the circulation of books and pamphlets, not only for the camp-ground, as was being done at the present time, but for years previous the country had been flooded with Millerite literature, pamphlets and books. No household on the South Side escaped this affliction. Many of the pamphlets were made up of labyrinthian diagrams and signs, with a muddle of mathematics, chronology, and Scripture references — entirely beyond the comprehension of any sane man. The devotion of these deluded people to their cause, and their absolute faith, transcends anything we have ever seen in the way of religious enthusiasm. In all their prayer-meetings, in their singing, and their conversations, there was an earnestness marvellous for so weak a cause. . . . Many proselytes were made in Hempstead from the sturdy, hard-working yeomanry of the South Side, who had successfully resisted the appeals of all other sects."

The two following letters written to the author's maternal grandmother, Mrs. George Peabody, of Salem, Massachusetts, give an account of a camp-meeting held in that city when it was at the height of its culture, distinction, and prosperity, and when William Miller's prophecy was one of the great points of discussion all over the country. It so happened that Mr. George Peabody and his family were in Europe when the great Tabernacle tent was pitched in North Salem and they received many interesting letters from relatives and friends at home, telling of the religious excitement that was sweeping the land. The first letter is as follows:

*Charles M. Endicott to his cousin, Mrs. George Peabody*
"SALEM, *Jan.* 5, 1843.

"We are in the midst, dear Clara, if not of a revolution, at least of a great excitement upon the subject of religion. Your previous letters from home have no doubt informed you that the Millerites have held a camp-meeting in North Salem, near Orne's Point, for upwards of a week, and our little city was daily about deserted. Large crowds were seen wending their way in that direction, and the roads were literally blocked up with carriages of all descriptions, conveying passengers to and fro from the place of meeting. I doubt if even Paris itself often presents a more busy scene. Their success in making converts was, I understand, quite satisfactory, and they proved, as conclusively as the Signs of the Zodiac multiplied by the seeds in a winter squash can prove anything, that this mundane orb of ours — the great 'Moulin Joly' on which we reside — will be extinguished, utterly destroyed, totally annihilated in April, 1843.

"Next came the great religious agitator, Elder Knapp, to what he was pleased to call 'this stronghold of Satan,' [1] and the way he dealt with his subtle Majesty, and the familiar terms on which he appeared to be with him, made many of his hearers feel more sensibly his immediate proximity than perhaps they had ever felt before; — the very brimstone flavor of his person was apparent to the olfactory nerves of many, and they involuntarily shuddered when they looked over their shoulders, lest they should encounter him with his pitchfork, ready to toss them into endless torments. Next to him and following close upon his footsteps came the more refined Mr. Kirk — with his persuasive eloquence and ornate rhetoric — administering to us in a more insidious manner, and in smaller doses at a time, the same kind of medicine, but more suited to those whose delicate stomachs

[1] N.B. There were a great many Unitarians in Salem at this time; most of them very antagonistic to Miller's doctrine.

refused the powerful potations of his predecessor; but having gained for himself considerable renown for his success in opening the eyes of the blind, particularly among the fashionables in Boston, he was of course much sought after, and much admired. However, we being a perverse and wicked generation, it did not last long — or, in other words, it was a total failure so far as those were concerned against whom this imagery was intended to operate: namely, the Unitarian denomination. At the same time with this polished divine, our city was favored with a visit from the erudite Mr. [Theodore] Parker, the transcendentalist, who had been delivering a course of sermons in the Mechanics Hall, to overflowing audiences. I humbly hope some good will come out of all this commotion, or awakening, as it is usually called, yet I cannot help having my misgivings that many pious and good resolutions will pass away with the occasion that called them forth. There has ever been in the world too much of that religion which Rebecca, in 'Ivanhoe,' said 'was forever on the tongue, but seldom in the heart, or in the practice.'

"I am, etc.

"Your Cousin

"C."

Another letter describing this same camp-meeting in more detail was received by Mrs. George Peabody from her brother, Mr. William P. Endicott:

"Salem, *December* 30, 1842.

". . . During the last fall and this much of the winter, signal and desperate efforts have been made for the conversion of sinners. First, Miller, the 'Prophet,' pitched his tabernacle in our neighborhood, and mighty was the struggle with Satan. The public exercises were unexceptionable, as I thought, but the family, or private, directions of his ignorant disciples, were inconceivably revolting. From attendance on these latter no one was excluded until the tent was full. I will give one instance of their general character. I was at the door of one of their tents, where a furious, ignorant fellow was praying for the sinners present in this wise: 'Oh, Sinners, the end is at hand and ye believe it not! Oh, repent before it is too late, for the end is coming! — and if He find you in your sins, better for you had you never been born, for He will swallow you in his wrath, and as you are fit for nothing but a vomit for Jehovah, when He has swallowed you He will spew you right up into hell!' — This is verbatim the language used, and, strange as it may seem, these impious ravings had the effect to add largely to the number of his followers. Scarcely had Miller blown his blast, when Elder Knapp, of Boston notoriety, took up the cry, and is now laboring night and day — not in my opinion to reform, but to proselyte, and well does he succeed. I cannot give a detailed account of the various machinery which is called into action. The most prominent, however, is the 'Anxious Seat,' to which many of the convicted sinners daily resort, and having gone through the purgation in such cases provided come out inexpressibly happy in the delusion that their work is done. Some, I doubt not, are truly benefited by the process; but is it not to be feared that many, if not most of them, sadly mistake in supposing that a few days of frantic consciousness of sin can atone for an ill-spent life? I have listened to this preacher, and can see much in him to explain the wonderful power he holds over the minds of the ignorant. He is a bold, unscrupulous denouncer of God's vengeance on all of a different faith. He excels in terrific descriptions of hell and torture; he opens the abyss, and his graphic language points the mind's eye to material torments and their infliction by the Devil, who, with his horn, hoof, and tail, rises to their terrified view, and so intensely horrible does he make the picture that many have, after a yell of despair, swooned away. His prayers are, in my opinion, blasphemous for their familiarity. For instance, he says: 'Send down, O Lord, the showers of thy grace upon this assembly, like unto a shower of fifty-sixes!' Of the Episcopalians he says: 'Their worship is so cold and formal, that a few of their prayer-books thrown into hell would freeze it over, so that the Devil would have good skating.' Of the Unitarians he says: 'Their steeples should point downwards, in order to give a correct idea of where the people are bound.'

"So you see if we are not all made better by the time you return to us, 'twill not be through want of rousing preaching. Mr. Kirk is here; — a different man altogether, etc., etc.

"Your affectionate brother

"W. P. E."

It is evident that Prophet Miller's health was still impaired at this time, as no reference is made in either of these letters to his preaching other than that after he had "blown his blast" he was succeeded by Elder Knapp and the more refined Mr. Kirk, both of whom seem to have made a definite impression, to say nothing of the fire-eating brother from the slums. That these men of such different calibre should be preaching in the same tent and almost at the same time to crowds of equally varying types shows how quickly and unerringly a definite and strongly worded suggestion will take hold of the imagination of the educated and uneducated alike — at least exciting curiosity if nothing else. At the age of ninety-three Mr. Daniel Kinsley, of Worcester, gave the author an account of a meeting he went to in Fletcher, Vermont, where William Miller preached. Mr. Kinsley was fifteen years old at the time. The meeting took place in a wood outside the village. It was a very fine day in June and a great crowd gathered there, arriving from all the neighboring towns and villages in traps and wagons.

When Prophet Miller mounted the platform, he appeared to be a little under medium height. Mr. Kinsley described him as being "a serious, earnest man with a wonderful power of holding the attention of his audience and of bringing them round to his belief. He did not shout or rant the way so many revivalists do; he made his impression by his earnest manner and his serious way of addressing his listeners. When he talked, people had to sit right up and listen — they couldn't help it."

Mr. Kinsley also said that many men who one would never suppose would be influenced by him or his theory would often be converted at once and get completely under the spell of the delusion.

Another account of a meeting where Prophet Miller preached was received by the author from Mrs. Susan L. Harris, of West Millbury, Massachusetts.

"I am eighty-two years old," she wrote, "and at that

time only five years of age; but hearing my mother in after years tell of it, it seems as though I remember it for myself.

"My mother at that time was living in Chicopee, near Springfield, in the western part of the State. Miller himself came there and held quite a number of meetings, and interest in the Second Coming of Christ ran fever heat.

"My mother, hearing so much said, attended some of the meetings herself. I remember of her telling of going to one, and while excitement ran high, ladies stripped ear-rings from their ears (they were quite fashionable in those days), and rings from their fingers, and sitting beside my mother was my oldest sister wearing my mother's gold beads, and she began to unfasten them to put in the collection when a timely nudge from my mother, and a hint to let her beads alone, stopped the programme.

"I remember, too, of hearing her say on the day appointed they assembled on a high hill near at hand robed in white, expecting to be of that class who are to meet the Lord in the air, but I think they must all be sleeping quietly in cemeteries by this time."

> "But in what awful sounds
> The wicked are addressed!
> Heaven with their groans resounds
> As on his left they're placed —
> 'Depart, ye cursed,' the Judge exclaims,
> 'To be destroyed in burning flames!'" [1]

[1] From *The Millennial Harp*. Published by Joshua V. Himes, 1843.

# CHAPTER VII

## THE BUILDING OF THE TABERNACLE

> "Hark, the Sinner thus lamenting
> At the thought of future pain;
> Cries, and tears he now is venting,
> But he cries and weeps in vain; —
> Greatly mourning
> That he ne'er was born again."
>
> *The Millennial Harp*, 1843

APRIL passed, and the earth, instead of being torn asunder and swept by fire, donned her garments of spring and burst into leaf and song.

At first there was evidence of surprise and disappointment among the Millerites, but it quickly gave way to renewed confidence. "After all," they reminded one another, "there is a whole year in which to look for the Coming; — we looked for it too soon, that was all" — and the singing and exhorting took on a new fervor.

While all this had been going on, a great wooden structure known as the Millerite Tabernacle was in process of building on Howard Street, Boston, the site being the same on which the theatre known as the Howard Athenæum stood in later years. The building was circular, about one hundred and fifteen feet in diameter, and so arranged as to hold several thousand people. This was the great rallying-point of the Millerites in Boston and the suburbs, and the public, whose curiosity in regard to their doings knew no bounds, kept incessant watch upon it. There was a story current that the building had been insured for seven years, but a denial of this appeared in "The Midnight Cry" of May 18, 1843, as follows:

"The false statement that the Tabernacle in Boston has been insured for seven years has been repeated by many newspapers. We are authorized by the Secretary of the Committee to say the building is insured for one year, as a matter of necessity, for the security of payment of expenses. A company offered to insure it for seven years, but the offer was declined."

The idea of building a Tabernacle germinated in the fertile brain of Elder Joshua V. Himes. It was to have been finished early in the year, but delays protracted the work, and it was not dedicated until May 6, 1843.

The dedication took place in the presence of a huge audience, and as Prophet Miller was very ill at the time Elder Himes was the grand master of ceremonies.

It needed a shrewd and quick mind like his to deal with the situation, which was a somewhat delicate one. April had passed, and Miller's followers as well as the public were very evidently awaiting some sort of explanation. Instead of delivering the address himself, Elder Himes laid that task upon the Reverend S. Hawley, a former Presbyterian clergyman who had become a convert, and who could be relied upon to bring out in strong relief certain statements which Elder Himes wished emphasized. In referring to the question concerning the coming of the end, every word was carefully chosen, as the following extract will show:

"With regard to that event, we expect it in 'the fulness of time'; in the fulfilment of all the prophetic periods, none of which have yet been shown to extend beyond A.D. 1843.

"And I stood upon the sand of the sea, and saw a beast rise up out of the sea, having seven heads and ten horns, and upon his horns ten crowns, and upon his heads the name of Blasphemy."

"And behold a great red dragon, having seven heads and ten horns, and seven crowns upon his heads. And his tail drew the third part of the stars of heaven, and did cast them to the earth."

ILLUSTRATIONS IN THE MIDNIGHT CRY

We are therefore looking for it at this time. Six thousand years from creation was the time when the primitive church was expecting the Advent, and Luther, Bengal, Burnet, Fletcher, Wesley, and others, all had their eye at about this period of time. And now the fulfilment of the prophecies and the end of the prophetic periods, and the signs of the times, admonish us that it is truly at the doors."

Following this came a statement which certainly must have astonished the audience, especially those who had been attending the camp-meetings in the early part of the year:

"The public has been deceived by the secular and religious press with regard to the particular days and months that it is said the Saviour was expected. There are too many difficulties in the way of fixing with certainty on any particular day to render it safe to point to such with any degree of positiveness, although to some minds more probable circumstances may seem to point to some particular days than others. When these days have been named by our Brethren they have been only their own individual opinions, and not the opinion of their friends. The cause is therefore not responsible for any such limited views and calculations. We occupy the same ground we have always occupied, in accordance with the title-page of all Mr. Miller's lectures, viz. — that the Second Advent will be about the year 1843. The 23d of April, to which all our opponents have looked, was never named by any of our friends — but only by our enemies.

"We should avoid all extravagant notions, and everything which may tend to fanaticism. God is not the author of confusion. 'Let everything be done decently and in order,' says the Apostle."

The Tabernacle Committee then made this specific statement, though it was soon forgotten in the agitation of the succeeding months:

"We are commanded to occupy until Christ comes. We are to sow our seed and gather our harvests so long as God gives us seed-time and harvest. If we improve the coming seed-time, and have no harvest, we shall have done our duty, and if a harvest should be granted us, we shall be prepared to reap. It is as much our duty now to be continually employed, either in providing for the wants of those dependent upon us, or in alleviating the distress of others, as it ever was. We are to do good as we have the opportunity, and by no means spend our time in idleness. That would bring reproach on our Saviour. Let us see to it that our hearts are right in the sight of God, and then, whether we wake or sleep, are laboring to save souls or are engaged in our daily avocations, we shall meet our Lord in peace. May the God of peace give all who profess to love His appearing, that wisdom that shall guide us aright, and lead us in the way of all truth, and redound the most to His honor and glory.

[Signed]    "PRESCOTT DICKINSON
"FREDERICK CLAPP
"WM. M. HALSTAT
"STEPHEN NICHOLS
"JOHN LANG
"MICAJAH WOOD
"JOSEPH G. HAMLIN
"JOHN AUGUSTUS
"JOSHUA V. HIMES
"Tabernacle Committee."

Having settled these points to the apparent satisfaction of Miller's following, Elder Joshua V. Himes and his committee held daily meetings at the Tabernacle in which the crowds filled every available space. The singing could be heard for a long distance, and those unable to gain entrance to the building thronged the streets outside. In all this agitation one psychological fact was brought out very clearly, and that was the entire inability on the part of the crowds as well as on the part of most of Miller's followers to take in so stupendous and overpowering a thought as the sudden appearing of our Lord — the earth dissolved in flames, the lightning change from this material world to either heaven or hell. Lips could utter the words, but brains failed to register them, consequently the behavior of the scoffing crowds and that of the believers were often inconsequent to the last degree. To exemplify this, while the meetings were going on in the Tabernacle, there was a general impression outside that during the meeting the Millerites expected to rise through the roof and float heavenward, and a great concourse of people would gather on the Common in the hope of catching a glimpse of them after they had risen above the intervening buildings and were well on their way. This is no fairy tale — it is a fact. The author of this book has a relative whose father was taken to the Common as a small boy "to see the Millerites go up" on one of these occasions!

On the 28th of May, Prophet Miller's son wrote the following lines to Elder Himes: "Father's health is no better, on the whole. He continues very weak and low, confined to his bed most of the time."

During this period and through the summer he was too ill

to take any part in what was going on, and Elder Himes had it all his own way; — or at least tried to. He could not have it with the Reverend John Starkweather, who continued to go about casting his mesmeric influence over unsuspecting audiences, and who appeared at a camp-meeting which commenced on the 9th of August, 1843, at Plainfield, Connecticut, where, according to Miller's biographer, "some manifestations were exhibited which were entirely new to those present, and for which they could not account."

But it did not need Brother Starkweather now to incite abnormal conditions. At Stepney, near Bridgeport, that same month, Elder Bliss tells us that some young men, professing to have the gift of discerning spirits, "were hurried into great extravagances."

Later on, in September, an article protesting against the actions on this occasion appeared in "The Midnight Cry," signed by Elder J. Litch:

"A more disgraceful scene under the garb of piety," he writes, "I have rarely witnessed. For the last ten years I have come in contact nearly every year, more or less, with the same spirit, and have marked its developments, its beginnings, and its results; and am now prepared to say that it is evil, and only evil, and that continually. I have uniformly opposed it wherever it has made its appearance, and as uniformly have been denounced as being opposed to the power of God, and as resisting the operations of the Spirit. The origin of it is the idea that the individuals thus exercised are entirely under the influence of the Spirit of God, are His children, and that He will not deceive them or lead them astray; hence every impulse which comes to them is yielded to as coming from God, and, following it there is no length of fanaticism to which they will not go." [1]

By this time all sorts of rumors were circulating in regard to the money which was being taken in by Elder Joshua V. Himes through his publications, and from collections taken at the camp-meetings, etc., which the public estimated as reaching large sums. As a matter of fact, a large percentage of the pamphlets he published were distributed gratuitously which cut down the receipts considerably. To be sure, the sale of Miller's lectures must have been large as well as the sale of "The Midnight Cry," but the expenses were heavy. There was the building of the Tabernacle, and the constant transportation and erection of the huge Tabernacle tent which was such a feature in aiding to spread Prophet Miller's doctrine; there were the expenses of travelling here and there and everywhere incurred by a very large number of preachers who were not able to pay their own way. These things the public did not take into account. There was also a rumor that as a proof that Prophet Miller did not believe his own prophecy, a high stone wall was being built about his farm. There are two accounts of visits made to his home which are interesting. One entirely contradicts the other. The first is an extract from a letter which appeared in "The Midnight Cry" of July 6, 1843, signed by A. Spaulding, and tells of going to see Miller during his illness:

"I had been there but a short time when he manifested his hospitality by inquiring if my horse had been taken care of. We freely exchanged views on the prophecies and conversed on the Coming of our Lord. . . . I said to him that I

[1] *The Midnight Cry*, September 14, 1843.

had not seen the high wall around his farm that I had so often heard of. He said that Mr. Tilden, who was present, would go with me to look for it. So we took a walk round the farm. There is some common stone wall, like that on all the farms in the vicinity. The land being stony and uneven, it is as cheap as any other fencing. Though his farm does not bear the marks of neglect, I saw no recent improvements, except one common gate. The buildings are in good condition, and everything in order. It is worked by his sons, plain, industrious farmers, who support his family and pay him a small sum yearly for his personal expenses. His house, like a number of others in the neighborhood, is a good two-story house with green blinds, and front and ends painted white. The furniture is plain, being all made for use, not for ornament. I saw nothing extravagant. In one room is a shoemaker's bench, used by one of his sons, who is a cripple.

"Brother Miller occupies one of the lower front rooms, where he has his bed, a few common chairs, his old bookcase, and a clock. In the other room is a portrait, painted some twenty years ago; a large diagram of the vision of Daniel and John, painted on canvas some like the miniature one in the last part of his book. The most elegant article in the house was a Bible, presented by a friend in Boston.

"The farm with its improvements is the product of many years of hard labor and economy. Everything connected with it seems to indicate that he believes what he preaches. He worked on his farm, studied his Bible, became convinced of the truth, and then declared it fearlessly to his fellow-men (travelling in most cases at his own expense), and they have in return said all manner of evil against him falsely."

The other letter appeared in the "Troy Times" of July, 1894, containing an account by the Reverend Professor Wentworth, then in the Troy Conference Academy, of a visit made by him to Prophet Miller on the day before the great expected conflagration. He states in it that, "although the final judgment was so near, and the faithful were casting away their worldly goods in contempt of all things perishable, it was not so with Miller himself. He believed in the Scripture injunction, 'Occupy till I come,' and his fields were clean-mowed and cropped, his woodhouse was full of wood sawed and piled for winter use. Forty rods of new stone wall had been built that fall, and a drag stood ready with boulders as a cargo to be laid upon the wall the next day." [1]

It is possible that Prophet Miller's sons who ran the farm thought it best to err on the safe side!

By September Miller had so far recovered his health as to enter the field of action again, and he made quite an extended tour in New Hampshire, taking in the towns of Claremont, Springfield, Wilmot, Andover, Franklin, Guilford, Gilmantown, Concord, and Exeter. From there he came into Massachusetts and lectured in Lowell; finally ending up with three lectures in Boston, after which he returned to his home in Low Hampton to rest.

During his sickness he had had no opportunity of discovering the spread of the fanaticism which had by this time become a serious problem wherever his followers congregated. On this last visit to Massachusetts, however, he came face to face with conditions that surprised and troubled him, and

[1] Daniel Treadwell, *Personal Reminiscences of Men and Things on Long Island.*

he wrote a letter of protest which was published in "Signs of the Times" on November 8, 1843.

"My heart was deeply pained during my tour," he writes, "to see in some few of my former friends a proneness to wild and foolish extremes and vain delusions, such as working miracles, discerning of spirits, vague and loose views on sanctification, etc. As it respects the working of miracles, I have no faith in those who pretend beforehand that they can work miracles. Whenever God has seen fit to work miracles, the instruments have seemingly been unconscious of having the power, until the work was done. They have, in no instance that I recollect, proclaimed as with a trumpet that they could or would work a miracle. Moses and the Prophets were more modest than these modern pretenders to this power. You may depend upon it, whosoever claims the power has the spirit of the Anti-Christ. The discerning of spirits is, I fear, another fanatical movement to draw off Adventists from the truth, and to lead men to depend on the feeling, exercise, and conceit of their own mind, more than on the word of God. . . . I have observed that those persons who think they have been baptized by the Holy Ghost, as they term it, become more sensitive of themselves, and very jealous of their own glory; less patient, and full of denunciatory spirit against others, who are not so fortunate as themselves. There are many spirits gone out into the world, and we are commanded to try the spirits."

But even Prophet Miller — the man who had sown the seeds of this fanaticism — had not sufficient power to prevent the rank weeds that sprang from them spreading their tentacles in all directions and smothering the growth of

"And behold a fourth beast, dreadful and terrible, which was diverse from all the others and exceedingly dreadful."

"I considered the horns, and behold there came up among them another little horn, before whom there were three of the first horns plucked up by the roots."

ILLUSTRATIONS IN THE MIDNIGHT CRY

healthy vegetation within reach. He emerged from his seclusion of many months of illness to find that his followers had pushed forward in his absence and had gone far beyond him. Moreover, they were now being directed by a host of other preachers of the doctrine, especially Elder Joshua V. Himes, who was the editor of the various newspapers and pamphlets promoting the Advent cause, thus controlling the reading matter meted out to the faithful, and who did little to stay this excess of fanaticism while professing to deplore it.

A few extracts from "The Midnight Cry" will give an idea of the way the doctrine was being spread:

"Charles Fitch, formerly pastor of the Free Presbyterian Church, Newark, New Jersey, will preach on the Second Coming of Christ at Hand, at the corner of Catherine and Madison Streets, next Sabbath morning. His stay in New York will be short. A collection will be taken to defray his expenses in the West." [1]

"Rev. Mr. Thimball will deliver a discourse on unfulfilled Prophecy next Sunday evening in the large Chapel of the New York University, Washington Square." [New York.] [2]

"Lectures will be continued three times on the Sabbath at the Apollo Hall, 410 Broadway, and at Columbia Hall, 263 Grant Street on Monday, Tuesday, Wednesday, and Friday evenings. Prayer Meeting will be held on Thursday evening at several private dwellings." [New York.] [3]

"Second Advent Camp-Meeting on the farm of Michael N. Stoner (*if time continues*) about one and one-half miles

---

[1] *The Midnight Cry*, June 1, 1843.
[2] *Ibid.*, June, 1843.   [3] *Ibid.*, June 3, 1843.

from Middleton, in sight of Harrisburg & Lancaster Railroad Turnpike and Pennsylvania Canal, to commence on Friday, 28th of July, and continue ten days. All who love the appearing of the Lord are solicited to attend and bring with them their tents. Comfortable lodging tents will be provided for all who may come from a distance, and boarding can be had on the ground at the rate of $1.50 per week, or 12½ cents per meal.

"All disorderly persons are forbid coming *on* or *near* the camp-ground; and all kinds of articles of traffic, spirituous liquors, Wine, Porter, Beer, Cider, etc., as prohibited by law to be sold within three miles of any religious meeting. The strictest order will be required from all during the whole time of the meeting.

"The public generally are invited to attend."[1]

## THE CAMP-MEETING AT BUFFALO, NEW YORK

The editor, Elder Joshua V. Himes, says of it:

"On the Sabbath we had a large crowd of the citizens of the City and vicinity; and of all places I have yet visited with the Tent, I must say we were never greeted with greater respect, or had better order among the multitude than in this place. The impression made has been favorable and powerful. The whole city is roused. The people are anxious for light. We have distributed publications by the thousands, and they are being read in every part of the city."

"Brother Himes visited Toronto, Canada, on the 9th instant. Arrangements were made for Brother Fitch to

[1] *The Midnight Cry*, July 27, 1843.

give a course of lectures in that city about the first of September." [1]

"Our next general move will be in Ohio — probably in Cincinnati, or vicinity, or where the Brethren may judge best. We intend if permitted to meet with our Brethren in that part of the country, to distribute about $2000 worth of publications in that part of the Union. We shall supply every town with a library as far as practical. We intend also to furnish all the ministers, *who will read on the subject*, with publications. If they cannot furnish them themselves, *we will furnish them.* They shall be left without excuse.

"We hope to see one mighty gathering in the West. Several efficient teachers will be there to lay before the people the strong reasons we have for our glorious hope." [2]

"Brother Hutchinson writes that he is doing all he can to spread the Cry in Canada and other places. . . . Any assistance that can be rendered him will be gladly received.

"Camp Meeting at Groton, Massachusetts, about two miles from the village, on the main road from Groton to Keene, commencing August 15th. Able advocates of the doctrine will be present." [3]

As the months went by, the situation became even more tense for Prophet Miller's followers, and what with the excitement of camp-meetings, the singing and the exhortations, and the perpetual tremors of fear created by the hourly watching for the end, hysteria repeatedly crossed over the border-line into insanity, and the asylums became crowded

[1] *The Midnight Cry*, August 17, 1843.
[2] *Ibid.*, August 3, 1843.      [3] *Ibid.*, August 10, 1843.

with poor deluded men and women who were mentally unable to stand the strain. In a book entitled "Boston Notions," printed by Nathaniel Dearborn in 1848, and sold by W. D. Ticknor & Co., Boston, and Wm. A. Colman, Broadway, New York, an account is given of the Miller Movement in which the following statement is made: "Hundreds of these unfortunate fanatics are now in the hospitals, and in the official report from that of Worcester, the number there on account of religious frenzies nearly equals the number caused by intemperance."

There is an interesting article written by the late Festus C. Currier, of Fitchburg, under the title of "Observations on the Nineteenth Century," and which he read before the Fitchburg Historical Society in 1902. Having personally seen Prophet Miller and having heard him lecture, his statements are of distinct value. In commenting upon the many and pitiful cases of insanity noticeable during that period, he mentions an occurrence he witnessed on June 17, 1843.

"Late in the afternoon," he states, "I was returning from Boston where I had been to the celebration of the completion of Bunker Hill Monument, and to hear Daniel Webster and see President John Tyler (who was a guest of the Monument Association). Riding on the outside of a stage-coach when passing along the street near the station of Wellesley Hills on the Boston and Albany Railroad, then known as Grantville Station, we observed four men carrying along in the direction of the station a man whom we supposed was drunk, or in a fit; but inquiry brought out the fact that he was being taken to the Worcester Insane Asylum.

The morning papers the next day reported the case. He was represented as a man about fifty years of age, in good standing and circumstances, but under the influence of Miller's doctrine had become hopelessly insane. This was only one of many unfortunates reported led away from reason and calm judgment. But the near approach of 'the last day,' as Miller termed it, only increased the excitement, and many substantial citizens were affected by it, particularly those of strong religious feelings and emotional temperaments."

If those of mature years were affected, children were no less so. In a sermon preached by the Reverend James A. Hayne in the Congregational Church in South Wilbraham during that period, he told the following anecdote as a warning to his parishioners in regard to the influence of Prophet Miller's prophecy on a child's mind.

"A little girl," he stated, "terrified by the talk of the world coming to an end and the burning up of the wicked, said, 'Mother I want to die this summer — I don't want to live next year and *be burnt up!*'"

An account of what children went through at that time appeared in "The Outlook" of May 18, 1908, written by Jane Marsh Parker who wrote from personal experience. Brother Marsh was a familiar figure in "The Midnight Cry," being quoted repeatedly, and his daughter's reminiscences, therefore, are doubly interesting. A few extracts will reveal the pressure under which these little people lived:

"I was six years old [A.D. 1843] when my father, the pastor of a country parish in eastern New York, 'came out of

Babylon,' burned his ships behind him, and moved his family to Rochester to fill the place designated for him by Father Miller as head of the western centre of the Movement, becoming the head of the weekly journal and of countless publications of the cause. His home was a port of storms for the travelling preachers, and their families as well, and its elastic hospitality included a large contingent of the faithful from the country roundabout, who had left their all to spend the remnant of time remaining in constant attendance upon the meetings of the believers. The prospect of 'all going up together with a shout' was ample compensation for sleeping on our parlor floor, as many had to do, and for leaving their babies overmuch through the day to the compulsory care of my mother's children.

"That the trumpet might sound any moment we children were in no danger of forgetting that summer, for, although a day had been set for the End, there was a possibility of another mistake in calculating periods; in misinterpretations, in missing links, etc. That it would not do to run any risks in disobedience was heavy on our infantile minds. We must do our best in caring for the babies left all too often on our hands. Dread expectancy of hearing the 'awful trump' became wonderfully dulled in the long tarrying — happily — but that the day was coming nearer that would burn as an oven, we never forgot. I knew what the heat of an old-fashioned brick oven was like — the sudden opening of a door of one had once singed my hair. I threw my rag doll upon a blaze of garden rubbish one day and, watching it shrivel to ashes, I learned what to be 'burned up root and branch' was like — and I with a green apple in my pocket that minute! 'If the Lord comes before morning, may I be caught up to meet Him in the air,' I never failed to say at night. Poor little Millerite! — 'Father would see that I was caught up in time out of the fire' (I said to myself), 'but then there were three of us little girls, and mother besides — and thunder and lightning always made her faint dead away.' Of course my kitten would have to go! — and a little boy I liked who said swear words! But these moods were brief, and came only when I had been very naughty. So all in all I did not have such a very bad time that summer, for there was no going to school, nor multiplication table, nor spelling book; — but then we had to read a good deal in our Bibles, and recite from a catechism on the Book of Daniel, making it plain as could be that the world was coming to an end that very year.

"I would give a good deal now to see one of those children's catechisms on Daniel prepared for the little Millerites. That there was also a textbook on the Apocalypse I am quite sure, for how else is my marked preference as a child for the vision of 'St. John' to those of the Book of Daniel to be accounted for? or my precocious acquaintance with all the *sevens* — candlesticks, angels, churches, seals, vials — each a well-spring for my imagination? — and with those locusts with lion's teeth and scorpion's tails, which relegated to the background even the fascinating he-goat of Daniel, who stamped not only upon the terrific ram, but the stars of heaven as well?

"'Going to Meeting' as much as we children did that summer (and oh! — so many fast days!) was wonderfully relieved by the rowdy scoffers who occasionally diversified the long sermons by noisy interruptions, when the police would arrive — always an impressive episode for us! Then sometimes a woman would fall into a trance and see strange things, or Brother Somebody would *speak with tongues* and have to be sung down! That we always enjoyed immensely. Or we had baptism by immersion in the river, when the great crowd upon the banks would sing

> "'You will see your Lord a-coming
> On the resurrection morning,
> While the band of music
> Will be sounding through the air.'

"Children used to rise for prayers in those big meetings, and tell their "speriences.' Mother advised our keeping out of that, and we did.

"Another feature was the great wooden image of Nebuchadnezzar's first dream that used to stand under Father Miller's pictorial chart of the prophecies — those grim portraitures of Daniel's dream and John's visions — beasts unknown to zoölogy! The image could be taken apart, kingdom by kingdom, until nothing was left but the feet of iron and clay, doomed to be broken in pieces 'on the tenth day of the seventh month of Jubilee!'...

"Telling stories, always from the Bible, like playing prayer-meeting, was a favorite pastime with the little Millerites. They always ended with these words: 'And that's the way the world is coming to an end 'tenth day of the seventh month, year of Jubilee!'

"The fate of Nebuchadnezzar was thereupon recited by us all in concert:

> "'He was driven from the sons of men;
> His dwelling was with the wild asses;

SYMBOLIC IMAGES
KING NEBUCHADNEZZAR'S DREAM

> He did eat grass with the oxen,
> And his body was wet with the dews of heaven
> Till his hair was grown like eagles' feathers,
> And his nails like bird's claws.'

"'Who is the king of the North?' we could tell with confidence; and 'Who is the king of the South?' The peculiar features of each of the terrible beasts — the woe of each vial — the names of the Hebrew children — the list of the musical instruments used at the dedication of the great image that the King of Babylon set up — how glibly we answered any questions of our catechism upon Daniel the Prophet!

"And the day went by and still the vision tarried. . . . Blessed is he that waiteth, Selah!"

A little anecdote revealing the simple credulity of a child's mind was obtained from Mrs. Theodore C. Parsons, of Agawam, Massachusetts, whose mother had many memories of the agitation created by William Miller's prophecy during the years 1843 and 1844 — her home being in South Scituate, Rhode Island, at that time.

There was a man named Barker who also lived there, who was an enthusiastic follower of the Prophet. One day a small boy was seen perched upon the fence in front of this good man's house, his wide-open eyes looking at it with a fixed stare. He sat there so long that some of the neighbors became curious, and one of them went across the road and asked him what he was looking at. The small youngster glanced up at her with a look in which fear, curiosity, and wonder were mingled. *"I'm waiting to see Mr. Barker go up!"* he whispered in awe-struck tones.

Another example of the fear hidden in the depths of

children's hearts during this period of agitation came from Miss Eugenie J. Gibson, of Woodsville, New Hampshire, whose uncle had many recollections of the excitement that prevailed in 1843 and 1844, as he was ten years old at the time. His family lived in a little village in southern Vermont.

"He was much impressed," Miss Gibson states, "with the neighbors' preparations for the day when the Angel Gabriel was to blow his trumpet. Many were selling their farms and stock (it never occurred to him to ask what they expected to do with the money!) and all were making white shrouds. He was much distressed at his mother's lack of interest, and one day begged to know when she was going to begin making their shrouds? When told she did not intend to make any, he decided the only thing for him to do was to keep near farmer Jones, who was big and strong, and hang on to his shroud when the signal came — ascending to heaven with him!"

Mrs. Paul Ruggles, of Camden, Maine, remembers her mother frequently telling of an experience she had when she took one of her little daughters to a Millerite camp-meeting in 1844, on which occasion men and women "threw themselves upon the floor — rolling around and shouting." Her poor child was so terrified, and screamed so wildly, that she had to be taken home.

Mr. John M. Fountain, of Eastport, Maine (who was born in 1835), requested his daughter to send the author the following amusing anecdote about himself as a child, when all were awaiting the end:

"He says he remembers the time very distinctly," so his

daughter wrote, "and he was a small boy, and that was all the people talked of, and much excitement was caused at the time. One thing he especially remembers is that he told his mother, as long as the world was coming to an end, why not kill all the chickens and hens, and have *a good feed before the time came?* She told him to shut up and keep still!"

> "Now, hark! the trumpet rends the skies;
> See slumbering millions wake and rise!
> What joy, what terror and surprise!
> The last Great Day has come!" [1]

[1] From *The Millennial Harp*. Published by Joshua V. Himes, 1843.

# CHAPTER VIII

## THE VERNAL EQUINOX

"Now despisers look and wonder,
Hope and Sinners here must part,
Louder than a peal of thunder
Hear the dreadful sound 'Depart!'
Lost forever!
How it quails the Sinner's heart!"

THE summer was drawing to a close, and as yet no sign of the end had come. Certain things had happened which had seemed to be of supernatural import to the expectant believers in the prophecy. There was the great comet flashing in the night skies; there was the jewelled Crown which some one claimed to have seen in the heavens, and the bloody moon, and the bloody sickle; and there had been a catastrophe at Rochester which had caused a great stir when a terrific gale of wind had caught up the huge Tabernacle tent into the air and had dropped it upon five hundred persons assembled there to hold a meeting, and not one of them had sustained serious injury, and this had been tabulated as a manifestation of special divine protection and an assurance of the approaching end; — but day after day passed by, and eager, anxious faces grew wan with waiting. Then a fluttering of doubt and hesitation became apparent in certain communities, but soon those were dispelled when it was recalled that as far back as 1839 Prophet Miller had stated on some occasion, which had been forgotten in the general excitement, that he was not *positive* that the event would take place during the *Christian* year from 1843 to 1844, and that he would claim the whole of the *Jewish* year which would carry the prophecy over to the 21st of March, 1844. An announcement to this effect was sent broadcast, and by this time the delusion had taken such a firm hold upon the imaginations of his followers that any simple explanation, however crude, seemed sufficient to quiet all doubts and questionings. The spell of the prophecy was drugging the natural perceptions of its victims.

Having accepted this lengthening of the allotted time, the brethren who had assumed the responsibility of sounding the alarm entered into their work with renewed energy and outdid themselves in their efforts to terrify the army of unbelievers into a realization of the horrors that awaited them and to strengthen the faith of those already in the ranks. But the months slipped by, one by one, and winter came, with its whirling snowstorms and blinding sleet, and fierce north winds — but still the "vision tarried."

The voices of the Millerites were heard singing and shouting and exhorting each other to stand firm, and to see to it that their lamps were trimmed and burning, ready for the awful moment whenever it might come. Still — nothing happened!

Little by little the days lengthened as the old earth rotated toward the vernal equinox, unmindful of man's prophecy of coming destruction; the sunshine grew warmer and buds began to swell; then the exaltation grew feverish and hectic, and the shouts grew strident.

Prophet Miller had been awaiting the end for weeks in his home at Low Hampton when the last day came — the 21st of March, which ended the Jewish year. Worn out by ill-health and premature infirmities of age, he waited in breathless suspense; reading and re-reading the Book of Daniel and consulting his chart; alert, and listening for the blast of the terrible trumpet which would awaken the sleeping dead. His confidence in the prophecy was unshaken; he looked for a final victory over the scoffers and detractors that had beset his path and flouted his doctrine, and he believed his reward was near — but the suspense was overpowering!

With Elder Joshua V. Himes it was different. He was working with indefatigable energy up to the end. The very morning of the 21st a large edition of "The Midnight Cry" was sent broadcast. In it he announced with startling inconsistency the arrival of the first number of a new paper called "The World's Crisis" in which were the following words of exhortation:

"Standing on the verge of the World's Crisis, in the very last moments of the period that is to witness the grand termination of all earthly things, we earnestly implore your prayerful perusal of these pages, as they contain some of the reasons for our faith that the present *Jewish year* will close up the drama of this earth, and usher in the scenes of eternity."

After quoting some of these reasons Elder Himes makes the following cautious announcement:

"To the Readers of The Midnight Cry.

"We have no new light on the *prophetic periods*. Our time ends this Jewish year. If time be continued beyond that, we have no other definite period to fix upon, but henceforth shall look for the event every hour till our Lord shall come. Others can give their views on the termination of periods on their own responsibility. If it be necessary, we shall give ours on this point.

"Let us be ready, having our loins girt about and our lamps burning, that when the Master cometh we may open to him immediately.

"J. V. HIMES.

"NEW YORK CITY."

Hour after hour through the day and through the night groups of deluded men, women, and children stood gazing heavenward watching the clouds, watching the sun, and later the stars — looking for the sign of the coming end. Some were terror-stricken; others worked themselves into a state bordering on frenzy, shouting Hallelujah! Hallelujah! — and some were dazed and could not speak.

But the dawn of March 22d crept over the sky, lighting up the pallid faces of the watchers. Once again the time had passed and the prophecy still remained unfulfilled; the end had not yet come.

Doubtless many even among the faithful inwardly rejoiced, but there were earnest souls among them to whom the realization of the cold fact was overwhelming!

How face the world now? — how face the *scoffers?*

Prophet Miller, enfeebled by the suspense and strain, and overcome by the shock of failure, remained in seclusion in his home at Low Hampton. After four days of semi-prostration, he aroused himself as from a stupor and wrote to Elder Himes:

"LOW HAMPTON, *March 25th*, 1844

" MY DEAR BROTHER HIMES:

"I am seated at my old desk in my east room, having obtained help of God until the present time. I am still looking for our dear Saviour, the Son of God from heaven. . . . The time as I have calculated it is now filled up and I expect to see the Saviour descend from Heaven. I have now nothing to look for but this glorious hope. I am full in the faith that all prophetic chronology, excepting the thousand years of Rev. 20 is now about full. Whether God designs for me to warn the people of this earth any more or not, I am at a loss to know. . . . I feel almost confident that my labors are about done; and I am with a deep interest of soul looking for my blessed and glorious Redeemer. . . . This I can truly say is my chief desire. . . . It is my meditation all the day long. It is my song in the night. It is my faith and hope.

"I still believe the time is not far off!"

The world made merry over the old Prophet's predicament. The taunts and jeers of the "scoffers" were well-nigh unbearable. If any of Miller's followers walked abroad, they ran the gauntlet of merciless ridicule.

"What! — not gone up yet? — We thought you'd gone up! Aren't you going up soon? — Wife didn't go up and leave you behind to burn, did she?"

The rowdy element in the community would not leave them alone.

Finally, on May 2d, Prophet Miller had recovered sufficiently to issue a statement which appeared in "The Midnight Cry." It was as follows:

"To Second Advent Believers.

"Were I to live my life over again, with the same evidence I then had, to be honest with God and Man, I should have to do as I have done. Although opposers said it would not come, they produced no weighty arguments. It was evidently guesswork with them; and then I thought, and I do now, that their denial was based more on an unwillingness for the Lord to come, than on any argument leading to such a conclusion.

"*I confess my error, and acknowledge my disappointment;* yet I still believe that the day of the Lord is near, even at the door; and I exhort you, my Brethren, to be watchful, and not let the day come on you unawares. The wicked, the proud, and the bigot, will exult over us. I will try to be patient. . . . I want you, my Brethren, not to be drawn away from the truth."

Prophet Miller's attitude in meeting this humiliating situation was noticeably different from that of Elder Joshua V. Himes. The former made no attempt to evade the responsibility of his miscalculations; he frankly admitted his mistake, and this very fact served to strengthen the confidence which his followers accorded him. The public also was not without appreciation of this when the Annual Conference met during the last week in May at the Tabernacle in Boston. The building was crowded to the doors by an audience that showed some sympathy for him, especially when, at the end of the Conference, he arose and, facing this great concourse of friends and foes, he spoke feelingly of his great disappointment. The "Boston Post" of June 1st gave an account of this occasion under the heading of "Father Miller's Confession." It reads thus:

"Many people were desirous of hearing what was termed 'Father Miller's Confession,' which, according to rumor, was to be delivered at the Tabernacle on Tuesday evening last, when and where a large concourse assembled, myself among the number, to hear the conclusion of the whole matter; and I confess I was well paid for my time and trouble. I should judge also, by the appearance of the audience, and the remarks I heard from one or two gentlemen not of Mr. Miller's faith, that a general satisfaction was felt. I never heard him when he was more eloquent and animated, or more happy in communicating his feelings and sentiments to others. . . . He confessed that he had been disappointed, but by no means discouraged or shaken in his faith in God's goodness, or in the entire fulfilment of His word, or in the speedy coming of our Saviour and the destruction of the world. 'If the vision tarry, wait for it,' he said. He remained firm in the belief that the end of all things is near at hand, even at the door. He spoke with much feeling and effect, and left no doubt of his sincerity." (Signed "D.")

There were many even among the scoffers who felt a certain sort of pity for the poor old Prophet on account of the frankness with which he admitted the error of his calculations, and the evident genuineness of his disappointment. Elder Joseph Litch went to see him on the 8th of June.

"That he is greatly disappointed in not seeing the Lord within the expected time," he wrote of him, "must be evident to all who hear him speak; while the tearful eye and subdued voice show from whence flow the words he utters. Although disappointed as to time, I never saw him more strong than now in the general correctness of his exposition of Scripture, and in the faith of our Lord's speedy coming." [1]

But in spite of the failure of the prophecy the fires of fanaticism increased. The flames of such emotions cannot be quenched at will; like all great conflagrations they must burn themselves out. And so it was in 1844. Instead of decreasing, the failure seemed to excite even greater exhibitions of loyalty to the expectation of the impending Judgment Day. Even before these deluded followers had wholly waked up to the situation, Brother Storrs, Brother Southard, Brother Snow, and a number of other preachers of the doctrine had consulted the great chart and the calendar of Jewish time, and the Books of Daniel and John, and the Apocalypse, and they made a discovery that the tenth day of the seventh month of the current Jewish year, which was the time of the barley harvest at Jerusalem, was the real and most probable time for the end to come. The instant this discovery was made, it was given out to the faithful, and though Prophet Miller refused to endorse it, they received it joyfully and greeted it with acclaim. With one accord and with feverish enthusiasm they threw themselves into a renewal of preparation for the end — poor souls! Elder Luther Boutelle described this period that led up to the final tragic disillusionment.

"By July," he states, "there was such a concentration of thought among the strong ones on time that it was called 'the Midnight Cry.' Thus a new impetus was created, and

[1] Sylvester Bliss, *Life of William Miller.*

the work of holding meetings and preaching was increased.
As we fell one after another into the current belief that the
fall would witness the coming of our Lord, it became in faith
a certainty — we believed with our whole souls. . . . The
time argument made the end in the fall of 1844, Jewish time,
tenth day of the seventh month, supposed to be October
20th — 21st — or 22d. This brought us to a definite time,
and in coming up to it the works of Adventists demonstrated
their faith and honesty, not to be questioned. As they moved
on with this point of time before them, all grew more enthusiastic. Crops were left unharvested, their owners expecting never to want what they had raised. Men paid up
their debts. Many sold their property to help others to pay
their debts, who could not have done it themselves. Beef
cattle were slaughtered and distributed among the poor.
At no time since the day of Pentecost was fully come had
there been the like — a day when that Pentecost was so
completely duplicated as in 1844.

"There was a great stir and talk in many places about
putting the Millerites under guardianship. But this did not
cause any to go back on their faith. They were firm and
held fast, believing they should speak and act. As the time
to which all looked drew near, the Bible was studied even
more, and a fuller consecration made."

This differs widely from Lydia Maria Child's caustic comment on the Millerites to the effect that she had heard of
very few instances of "stolen goods restored, or of falsehoods acknowledged, as a preparation for the dreaded
event." [1]

[1] Daniel M. Treadwell, *Reminiscences*.

In spite of her opinion, however, there were many more than would seem possible in this day, who, like Elder Boutelle, were earnest, sober, God-fearing men, notwithstanding their delusion. This good man belonged to a group of the Prophet's followers whose minds were filled with the devotional aspect of the experience; and that there was one (in spite of the scoffers) lends a note of pathos and tragedy to what from the outsider's viewpoint seemed only foolishness. These were the real Millerites, but in addition to these were two other groups, one of them composed of hysterical, terrified, heedless men and women, and the other counting those who merely craved excitement and morbid exhilaration.

The public at this time, seriously deploring the increase of insanity and fanaticism, gravely censored the actions and the influence of Elder Joshua V. Himes. The majority of those against the doctrine distrusted him, and there were some among Miller's followers who at times questioned his sincerity. In July an article signed "Delta" appeared in a paper called the "New Sun" protesting against the sale of his publications. "I learn from a notice in the 'Christian Reflector,'" this article states, "that this Unitarian editor, Joshua V. Himes, instead of endeavoring to repair the almost uncalculable mischief that he has caused among the churches of Christ for the last two or three years, by advocating a scheme of prophetical interpretations which time has shown to be false, has recently come out with a new speculation upon the credulity of his followers in the form of a quarterly pamphlet of 144 pages which he sells at 37½ cents per number. The following extract from the notice referred to will give an idea of the object, spirit, and contents of this pamphlet: 'The tenor and object of the whole work,' it asserts, 'is to keep alive by vigorous fanning the flames which gleamed so fiercely one or two years ago.'"

This was copied into "The Midnight Cry" of July 4, 1844, and scornfully reviewed by the editor, but that he was now beginning to be looked upon as the chief fomenter of trouble, owing to the tone of his publications, was very evident. Popular caricatures are apt to reveal the trend of public sentiment, and one which was published about this time and which is now in the possession of the Society for the Preservation of New England Antiquities in Boston, demonstrates the prevailing estimate of the two men, namely, William Miller and Elder Joshua V. Himes. This one in question depicts the Tabernacle Building in Boston in the act of being caught up into the air, from the roof and windows of which, miserable sinners, both men and women, can be seen falling through space to the place of torment, while serene and secure upon the peak of the roof sits Prophet Miller, his famous chart spread out beneath him. Below on earth is Elder Joshua V. Himes, his arms reaching upward in a frantic effort to catch hold of the building so as to ascend with it, but Satan holds him back with a firm grip, uttering the cryptic words: "*Joshua V., you must stay with me!*"

The fact that Elder Himes and Prophet Miller remained in the Middle West during the summer of 1844 left the field clear to the Eastern States for leadership on the part of some of the lesser lights among the Brethren, and that these took occasion to promulgate theories of their own is perhaps an explanation for some of the symbolism which became rampant during this period, certain manifestations of which will always be associated with the Millerite excitement of 1843 and 1844. Owing to the ridicule which was hurled at them on account of these acts of symbolism by a merciless public that kept it up for a long time after the wave of fanaticism had subsided, the exasperated and humiliated followers of the Prophet turned upon their persecutors after some years had passed, and declared that those things which excited their ridicule had never happened and were fabrications of their own brains. To be sure, there were many impossible stories current at the time which were entirely false, but there remain too many proofs of the truth about this period of undue agitation, from letters, and from recollections of those still living, and from authentic accounts of it, passed on from the generation then living to the next in line, and from writings of the Millerites themselves in the columns of their various publications, to admit of any uncertainty as to what really happened. Moreover, the kind of fanaticism that seized hold of Miller's followers resembled in almost every instance that indulged in at all similar outbursts when the end of the world had been looked for at intervals during preceding centuries. In almost every case the expression of this fanaticism was symbolic, except where mesmeric influence veered it off into morbid channels. Seeking the hilltops, the tree-tops, and the house-tops; the donning of white robes as the time of the expected end approached; the washing of each other's feet, greeting each other with a kiss — all these acts had esoteric meanings which had come down through the ages fraught with solemn beauty, but when performed by the unenlightened and the ignorant they seem like acts of meaningless absurdity. Now climbing into the tree-tops, which was much resorted to by the Millerites, undoubtedly had its origin in the natural and spontaneous act of Zaccheus in the New Testament who, we are told in St. Luke's Gospel, climbed up into a sycamore tree so as to catch a glimpse of the Master when he was passing through Jericho on his death journey to Jerusalem. It is safe to say, however, that most of Miller's deluded followers performed the act without knowledge of its origin, thinking only of the advantageous elevation secured from which to ascend when the end came. But to illustrate how such waves of religious hysteria wherever they vibrate will generate the same impulses, the Reverend C. V. A. Van Dyke, an Episcopal clergyman, who met the beautiful Harriet Livermore during her pilgrimage in Jerusalem, wrote in regard to her fanaticism to the Reverend St. Low Livermore: "I remember hearing Miss Livermore say that she had spent the preceding Sabbath in an olive tree on the Mount of Olives."

The hillsides and the summits have ever been regarded in the East as a refuge for meditation and prayer; and all through the eventful summers of 1843 and 1844 long processions of Millerites could be seen wending their way up the green slopes of some hill back of their town or village, there to await or watch out for the coming of the Lord. The habit of repairing to the roofs of houses to await the end was in accordance with the habit of the Eastern peoples who resort to the house-tops to recite their prayers at the rising and setting of the sun. As their roofs are flat, they are considered a fitting retreat for contemplation.

"Let him which is on the house-top not come down . . . and he that is in the field, let him likewise not return back." These words of warning in the twenty-fourth chapter of the Gospel of St. Mathew were literally followed in many cases, and poor deluded men and women crouched as best they could on the gutters of our slanting roofs — when they thought the end was near. But here again the scriptural application was in most cases lost sight of in a desire to get where they could be caught up in the air unimpeded by obstructions; at least it was surely so amongst the country folk. The symbolism of the white robes is, of course, very evident, as being emblems of purity.

"And lo, a great multitude, which no man could number, of all nations, and kindreds, and peoples, and tongues stood before the throne, and before the Lamb, clothed with white robes, and palms in their hands." [1]

"And one of the elders answered, saying unto me, What are these which are arrayed in white robes? And whence came they?"

They were also looked upon as the wedding garment spoken of in the parable of the marriage feast.

"And when the king came in to see the guests, he saw there a man which had *not* on a wedding garment: and he saith unto him, Friend, how camest thou in hither not having a wedding garment? And he was speechless. Then said the king to the servant, Bind him hand and foot, . . . and cast him into outer darkness." [2]

An explanation of this, written by J. Hamilton, of London, in a Millerite publication called "The Morning Watch," is as follows:

[1] Rev. VII, 9, 13.     [2] Math. XXII, 11-13.

"You will observe that a welcome from the King depends entirely on what the Gospel parable calls a 'wedding garment.' This robe, according to the custom of old and Eastern times, is provided by the lord of the house, and is put on every guest as he enters — of course only if he be willing; but no one who is willing need want it, for it is gratuitously given to all. The robe is Righteousness — not man's, but Jehovah's."

And so the Millerites, fearing to offend the Almighty, and longing to belong to that great company about the throne, made white garments for themselves — "ascension robes," they were often called — and they wrapped themselves in them when the end seemed near, just as other fanatics did before them in preceding centuries. Here and there in country districts black robes were used, but this was very unusual. These symbolized *humility*.

This explanation is an important one at this point, as from now on various accounts from authentic sources are full of references to these observances.

Now all through the summer, while Prophet Miller and Elder Himes were away in Ohio, the cry went up, "*Tenth day of the seventh month, year of Jubilee!*" It became a sort of slogan among believers as well as unbelievers of the doctrine. Even the "scoffers" took it up. Among the faithful, however, it stirred emotions such as they had never experienced before. Little did it matter to them now whether Prophet Miller or Elder Himes gave countenance to the new date settled upon. Every other self-elected Millerite preacher was shouting it so that all could hear, and the followers took it up in ringing tones, in defiance of reason, in defiance of the jeers of unsympathetic crowds; in defiance of those attempting to steady them, entreating them to keep balanced; in defiance of everything and everybody. When Prophet Miller and his co-worker Elder Himes turned their faces homeward and arrived in Philadelphia on September 14, 1844, they found their followers in a turmoil of excitement preparing for the end, every one of them repeating with burning conviction: *"Tenth day of the seventh month, year of Jubilee!"*

It was the same upon their arrival in New York on September 19th. The cry of *"Tenth day of the seventh month"* rang in their ears wherever they went. Exhausted by lecturing throughout Ohio, by illness and advancing years, the poor old Prophet was agitated and troubled. Elder Himes was worried. It was easy enough to see that during their absence the reins had been shifted into the hands of those who were now driving the Millerite chariot down a steep descent at breakneck speed. With practically only a month to wait before the arrival of the expected final day of earth, many were giving away their property, or selling their farms and possessions, urged on by some of the preachers who had worked themselves into such a condition of mental chaos that any attempt made to reason with them was useless. When Prophet Miller reached his home at Low Hampton, he found his courage almost failing him. He wrote to Elder Himes on September 30th:

"DEAR BROTHER:

"I am once more at home, worn down with the fatigue of my journey, my strength so exhausted and my bodily infirmities so great, that I am about concluding I shall never be able again to labor in the vineyard as heretofore. I wish now to remember with gratitude all those who have assisted me in my endeavors to awaken the Church and to arouse the world to a sense of their awful danger. . . . Many of you have sacrificed much — your good names, former associates, flattering prospects in life, occupation and goods; and with me you have received scorn, reproach, and scandal from those whom it was our soul's desire to benefit. Yet not one of you *to whom my confidence has ever been given*, has, to my knowledge, murmured or complained. . . . There have been deceivers amongst us, but God has preserved me from giving them *my confidence* to deceive or betray."

Elder Boutelle describes this period thus: "The 'Advent Herald,' 'The Midnight Cry,' and other Advent papers, periodicals, pamphlets, tracts, leaflets, voicing the coming glory, were scattered broadcast and everywhere like autumn leaves in the forest. Every house was visited by them. . . . They were angels of mercy sent in love for the salvation of man. Everything now began to converge to a point. October was the closing time of probation; the judgment and rewards! A mighty effort through the Spirit and the word preached was made to bring sinners to repentance, and to have the wandering ones return. All were awake to this great end — salvation. The tenth day of the seventh month drew nigh. With joy all the ready ones anticipated the day. Solemn, however, were the last gatherings. Those of a family who were ready to meet the Lord, expecting an eternal separation from those who were not ready. Husbands and wives, parents and children, brethren and sisters, separated, and that forever!"

The camp-meetings were now so crowded that they were no longer orderly as they had been. If there had been a time when an undesirable element could be kept out, it was now impossible to do so; and as a matter of fact the world was so near its end, as they claimed, whatever precautions were taken before seemed hardly worth while any longer. Brother Stoddard, who was preaching at a camp-meeting at Litchfield, Connecticut, wrote about his experiences there which were typical of what was happening at all such meetings in greater or lesser degree.

"On Saturday evening," he states, "the great enemy of our doctrine sent out about three hundred believers that the Lord delays his coming. They began to defend their doctrine by throwing apples and tobacco at the preachers in the stand, and after that engaged in mocking and blasphemy, and at a convenient time stoned to pieces the chandeliers and put out the lights, and after that broke the stand to pieces, and began to burn the boards; when the high sheriff and one of his deputies, being present, began to advise them to desist, with a little degree of earnestness, but were careful not to threaten them. We have learned the civil authority was under foot, and could not restrain the wicked even in Connecticut. We attended to our work, continued the meeting as long as we intended, and not a hair of our head was hurt." [1]

Brother E. L. H. Chamberlain in the same paper writes of

[1] *The Midnight Cry*, October 3, 1844.

this meeting: "It was a time of great power; much good was done. I don't think there was one preacher on the ground that did not come out fully on the seventh month. Awful moments these — and *it is so*, yes, the word and the Spirit agree, Glory to God! . . . I think I shall have to close my store, and let it, and preach the Lord is coming. This will be a heavy cross, indeed! My son is now in the store and wants me to warn the people!"

Now there were many whose inconsistences were as glaring as Brother Chamberlain's, who like him were cautious enough *to let their stores* even if they believed the end was near. It is difficult, after all, for some thrifty Yankees to become wholly oblivious to the advantage of making a good trade on the chance of needing it.

Mr. John Whitcomb, of Amesbury, Massachusetts, now in his eighty-seventh year, wrote to the author on November 28, 1921, of being taken to Fitchburg, Massachusetts, when a small boy.

"We went to Fitchburg to see some of father's folks, and Mr. Miller's folks had a big tent out of town, and they held meetings for a week, and some lived there, and the boys bothered them nights. One night they went up and they got a small boy and gave him a good sharp knife and told him they would throw him to the top of the tent, and when he got there to stick his knife through and it would hold him and he could hear all they said. So they threw him and he stuck his knife in the tent and down he came, knife and all, and slit the tent from the top to the ground. The wind blew in and blew out the candles, and when the lights were out they threw a pig in, and some had pork under them, and some over them for a while! It broke up the meeting for that night."

The following is a verse of an old Millerite camp-meeting hymn which was very generally sung at this period:

"Lo, what a glorious sight appears
To our believing eyes;
The earth and sea are passed away
And the old rolling skies!

*Chorus:*
"And the old rolling skies —
And the old rolling skies —
The earth and sea are passed away,
And the old rolling skies!"

# CHAPTER IX

## PERSONAL REMINISCENCES OF THE END

"T'is time we all awake;
    The dreadful day draws near;
    Sinners, your proud presumption check,
    And stop your wild career!"

*Millerite hymn*

No mere words can adequately express the breathless agitation, the appalling solemnity that filled the hearts of Prophet Miller's followers when the month of October came in. This time, in spite of no endorsement from him, they swept forward in solid ranks of conviction toward the new date which was close at hand. It seemed as if the adverse attitude of the unbelieving public was stirring a sort of desperate defiance among the poor deluded fanatics. They *would* believe; they *knew* that this time there was no mistake — the Lord was surely coming! — they would be justified! — they would be saved! — and all their tormentors would be cast into the burning lake, they would suffer eternally!

On October 3d Brother George Storrs wrote as follows in "The Midnight Cry": "I take up my pen with feelings such as I never before experienced. *Beyond a doubt* in my mind the *tenth day of the seventh month* will witness the revelation of our Lord Jesus Christ in the clouds of Heaven. We are then within a few days of that great event. Awful moment to those who are unprepared, but glorious to those who are ready! I feel that I am making the last appeal I shall ever make through the press. My heart is full. I see the ungodly

"And there came out . . . locusts upon the earth
. . . And the shapes of the locusts were like unto
horses prepared unto battle."

"And the fifth angel sounded, and I saw a star
fall from heaven unto the earth: and to him was
given the key of the bottomless pit."

SYMBOLIC ILLUSTRATIONS IN THE MIDNIGHT CRY
1843

and the sinner disappearing from my view, and there now stands before my mind the *professed believers* in the Lord's near approach."

In describing these momentous last days Elder Luther Boutelle wrote: "Such a concentration of thought; such a oneness of faith was never before witnessed; certainly not in modern times. All that did speak spoke the same things. Solemn, yet joyful. Jesus coming! We to meet him! Meetings everywhere were being held. Confessions made, wrongs righted; sinners inquiring what they should do to be saved. Those who were not with us were mightily affected. Some were exceedingly frightened with awful forebodings." [1]

"The Midnight Cry" of October 3d published a few words from Brother N. Southard under the heading "Confession":

"One of my besetting sins has been a desire to please those around me, instead of inquiring simply what would the Lord have me do, to be, and to say? I confess this before the world, but I cannot confess that I have not thought I was doing right in publishing the evidence of Christ's near coming. I have not been half awake to the greatness of the subject. May God forgive me in this thing, and grant me grace to be *wide awake* till He comes. Dear Reader, are you awake? If not, it is high time to wake out of your sleep!"

Poor Brother Southard, he was bound to make everything all right as far as he was concerned before the Great Day should come, for on another page of this same issue of "The Midnight Cry" under the heading of "Notice," is

[1] *Life of Elder Boutelle.*

the following: "If any human being has a just pecuniary claim against me, he is requested to inform me instantly."

Another brother exhorts every one of the faith to keep their "robes unspotted," and to dwell in love, and to be dead to the world.

Another writes: "See that you have on the *true ascension robe* — the holiness without which no man shall see the Lord!"

And still another: "We are living now at an awful point of time! Say, Brethren! have you done all your duty to your relatives, your friends, and the world? Is your all upon the altar? Are you there? — are your talents — your property there? *Time is almost gone!*"

One contributor, filled with awe and wonder, draws attention to how the ancient prophecies were one by one being fulfilled, and has for a heading "The Potato Crop":

"How painful it is to learn that whole crops of this valuable esculent have been destroyed by the rot. The only section from which little complaint is heard is Maine, but even there the crop has not escaped the disease."

This is like what the Prophet Haggai speaks of: "*Ye looked for much and it came to little!*" [1]

One exchange paper also says: "The diseased potatoes are said to be poisonous, and to have caused the death of hogs fed upon them."

The Prophet Joel saith: "*How do the beasts groan!*"

Whoever sent in this contribution further added: "We have neither time nor room to go over the prophecy fur-

[1] From the *Claremont Eagle.* (New Hampshire.)

ther. This little item is added to the everlasting evidence we had before."

Elder Himes had tried in vain to steady things by publishing the following facts in the columns of "The Midnight Cry," October 3d: "The impression has extensively prevailed that this year is observed as a Jubilee by the Jews. We have just called on Rabbi M. Isaacs, of this city, who referred to the Jewish calendar, and stated that the anniversary of the Jubilee would not occur for *twenty-five years yet*. They commence their year in the fall, and reckon this year commencing with the new moon, September 14th, to be the year 5605 from Creation, and their next Jubilee would not come till the year 5628."

But it was too late; he might as well have talked to the winds. "It will be the *Lord's Jubilee*, not the Jew's Jubilee," the followers cried.

And now he wrote again in a futile attempt to clear himself of responsibility for the surging wave of anticipation that was sweeping all before it: "Our readers may have noticed," he asserts, "that we have spoken with some hesitation in reference to the seventh month, though we have inserted the communications of brethren who were fully convinced that the Lord would come then."

Elder Himes evidently had no recollection of another statement he once made to the effect that an editor was responsible for whatever appeared in the columns of his newspaper. But for once in his life he was baffled. He did not know what to do, or how to cope with the situation. The public was denouncing him; on the other hand, the very men in whom he had helped to sow the seeds of religious hysteria were now looking at him questioningly, not understanding his attitude of aloofness. It is difficult to know what Elder Himes expected at the time when he did his best to wake up the sleeping brethren, but it is evident that he had not anticipated a situation like the present one.

Brother Storrs and Brother Snow and some of the other hallucinated brethren did not give him any time to think things over. They hurried with breathless eagerness to confer with poor, ailing, troubled, tired-out old Prophet Miller, announcing their conviction that this time his prophecy was sure of being fulfilled, and they explained first one point and then another to him to bear out their assertions, and before he knew it he was under the sway of their ecstatic enthusiasm, the smouldering hope within him flared into flames, and he was swept into the current of delusion again like a dried leaf caught in the whirling eddies of a stream. In three days' time he succumbed wholly to their arguments and signed an endorsement of them.

Then trembling with joy the deluded old man wrote the following hysterical effusion to the editor of "The Midnight Cry," October 12th:

"Dear Bro. Himes:

"I see a glory in the seventh month which I never saw before. Although the Lord had shown me the typical meaning of the seventh month one year and a half ago, yet I did not realize the force of the types. . . . Thank the Lord, O my soul! Let Bro. Snow, Bro. Storrs, and others be blessed for their instrumentality in opening my eyes! I am almost home. Glory! Glory! Glory! I see that the time is correct; yes, my brother, our time 1843 was correct. How so, say you? Did not the Lord say: 'Unto two thousand three hundred days, then shall the sanctuary be cleaned.' But when? When the seventh month comes. . . . That is the typical time; then will the people and place be sanctified. When did the twenty-three hundred days end? Last spring. Then the vision tarried. How long? Until the seventh month, and will not tarry another year, for if it should, then it would be twenty-three hundred and one years.

"But, bless the Lord! He has not deceived us. O my soul, how clear that it must tarry until the seventh month — it will not tarry beyond. I believe it, yes, I love it.

"Oh, the glory I have seen to-day. My Brother, I thank God for this light. My soul is so full I cannot write. My doubts and fears and darkness are all gone. I see that we are yet right . . . and my soul is full of joy; my heart is full of gratitude to God. Oh, how I wish I could shout; but I will shout when the King of Kings comes.

"Methinks I hear you say: 'Bro. Miller is now a fanatic!' Very well — call me what you please. I care not — Christ will come on the seventh month and bless us all. Oh, glorious hope! Then I shall see Him — and be like Him — and be with Him forever; — yes, forever and ever!

"WILLIAM MILLER."

The poor old man was broken in health and at times downhearted, but this renewal of his hopes stirred him and enraptured his soul. He examined his chart again with all the fervor of a blind enthusiasm. "If Christ does not come within twenty or twenty-five days, I shall feel twice the dis-appointment I did in the spring!" So he wrote according to his biographer, Elder Bliss.

All were falling in line now. "The Voice of Truth" of October 2d announced that Elders Marsh, Galusha, and Peavy, who considered themselves more conservative than some of the others, had given their full endorsement to the belief that the tenth day of the seventh month would usher in the end. Everything now became potent with meaning. Even the ordinary trivial happenings assumed a new ex-pression. But there were reports of unusual happenings that were whispered from mouth to mouth and these increased the agitation tenfold. Among these was the case of Sister Mathewson. On October 10th there are accounts of her in "The Midnight Cry," which led the followers to believe that supernatural agencies were at work.

A writer signing himself C. Morley gives the following account:

"Readers are you aware that the Lord is working a wonder in these days which has no parallel in the history of the world?

"In an obscure town in Connecticut a woman now lives who has been sick ten years and given up by skilful physi-cians to die. *She says she died*, and since then she has lived more than three times forty days and nights *without food*. This is a miracle which of itself should startle the world. It is a miracle wrought in these last days to confirm a message — a message of merciful warning that *time is short*. You may talk about superstition, but he must be madly unbelieving who does not see and feel that the finger of God is in this thing. If you can look at this matter with unconcern, you have reason to tremble for yourself."

George A. Stirling, an Elder, gives a more detailed account:

"I last week went to South Coventry, where in a very retired spot of this wilderness world I beheld this wonder. For a long time she had been so weak as to be unable to bear the least noise, so much so that *it was necessary to walk in the adjoining kitchen with shoes off.*

"Her dying sensations and pains commenced in her feet. When the pain reached the region of her heart, she broke into *very loud* singing, and sang for *five hours;* since which the noise has not affected her any more than one in the soundest health. This is a fact. This is supernatural. This is miraculous. It is the power of *God quickening a dying body.* Where is there a person in soundest health that can sing with perfect ease for five hours, loud enough to be heard in the whole of a large two-story house? She did it — yet not she, but God in her. This is the first fact.

"The second is, that she continues to this day in the same state, *without the use of any food,* testifying to all that 'time is short.' It is not simply a fact of forty days and nights, but it is a fact, even now, of over one hundred and twenty days and nights. She drinks half a cup of weak tea (cup of common size) twice a day, with the usual quantity of sugar and milk. At first an attempt was made to have her eat nutritious food, her friends not suspecting the mighty change that had come upon her.

"Where is there an individual who would be willing to attempt for all the wealth of the Indies to live half these number of days, taking only their usual quantity of tea, which she affirms she takes only for the moisture it contains, having no appetite for food? . . .

"The third fact is, that, during this long period of abstinence, there has been no perceptible change in the appearance of the quantity of flesh upon her frame; she in the beginning having become very poor, continues only so to the present, the expression of her eyes being sweet, placid, and heavenly.

"The fourth fact is this, that when her family became convinced of her miraculous state, and it was 'noised abroad,' there was a mighty gathering of the people, insomuch that they thronged the house from morning until night, sometimes two hundred a day. With these she had power to converse upon her change and warn them often from early morning till late at night; then she would spend much, if not all of the remainder of the night in singing, as she said, with angels, who encompassed roundabout her bed, whose shining bodies it was given her to behold and admire.

"These four facts are perfectly sufficient to prove her supernatural state. . . .

"A Baptist clergyman of the place has, for the satisfaction of others, given a public statement to the above, but *drew no conclusion from it!* O my God, the professed ministers, who say they are watching upon the walls, draw no conclusion from the most marvellous providences, than suits the Devil! O watchman, brother watchman, what of the night? This sister says first, *that she died;* second, that before her death her spirit was caught up and conducted by angels

"And the sixth angel sounded."

"And the seventh angel sounded."
This is the sound of the last trump, at
which the dead will rise.

SYMBOLIC ILLUSTRATIONS IN THE MIDNIGHT CRY
1843

to the gate of heaven. . . . The period of this absence was but for a moment at the close of which she died, in which state she continued about the space of half an hour, at the end of which she came to, having lost the memory of all things but that of her friends. Her mind being restored, she burst into tears, because, she said, 'I have got back to this wicked world.' She is perfect meekness, making no difference as to persons, but speaks equally to all high, low, rich and poor, in the spirit of a little child. Humbleness and wisdom seem to mark her course, so much so that all seems in perfect accordance with the idea of her message coming from a divine source. Glory be to God — I believe it! — I *know* it! — I will heed it by the *humbling*, quickening grace of God, and be ready on the tenth day of the seventh month of the present year (Jewish) when the great trumpet of Jubilee will *certainly sound!* . . ."

Whether it was Prophet Miller's sudden endorsement of the seventh-month theory, or whether it was that he was unable to retain any sort of equilibrium in the midst of so much hysterical hallucination, cannot be stated, but the following item which appeared in "The Midnight Cry" of October 10th records the Reverend Joshua V. Himes as a supporter now of the tenth day of the seventh month expectation:

"Brother Himes lectured Friday afternoon and evening at Chrystic Street, exhibiting the evidence of the Lord's coming on the tenth day of the seventh month, giving an account of the blessed effects of the doctrine."

Then in the issue of October 12th we find this letter:

"*To our Readers* —

"DEAR BRETHREN AND SISTERS:

"We find we have arrived at a most solemn and momentous crisis, and from the light we have, we are shut up in the conviction that the tenth day of the seventh month must usher in the glorious appearing of our great God and our Saviour Jesus Christ. We therefore find our work is now finished and that all we have to do is to go out to meet the Bridegroom and to trim our lamps accordingly. . . .

"We feel that we are now making our last appeal; that we are addressing you through these columns for the last time. In this crisis we must stand alone. If you are hanging upon our skirts, we shake them off. Your blood be upon your own heads. We ask forgiveness of God and all men for everything which may have been inconsistent with His power of glory; and we desire to lay ourselves upon the altar. Here we lay our friends and worldly interests.

"J. V. HIMES."

It is interesting to note that on this same date the "Boston Post" gives out this warning: "The public indignation is so much excited against Himes that we think it would be prudent for him to give a general notice of his movements."

This was undoubtedly due to the fear for the sanity of those now taking part in the meetings at the Tabernacle on Howard Street, where evidences of the stress of mind under which many were laboring were only too apparent. As the date approached, frightened men and women from the outlying districts crowded into Boston from a desire to be under the roof of that strangely constructed edifice and to "go up" with the multitude collecting there. And here, as well as at every other gathering place of the faithful, these terrible words of Prophet Miller were now read, while men and women cowered in fear, and covered their faces with their hands:

"But you, O impenitent men and women, where will you be then? When heaven shall resound with the mighty song, and distant realms shall echo back the sound, where, tell me where, will you be then? *In hell!* O think! *In hell!* O dreadful word! Once more think! *In hell!* lifting up your eyes, being in torment. Stop sinner, think! *In hell!* where the beast and false prophet are, and shall be tormented day and night, forever and ever. I entreat you to think — *In hell!* I know you hate the word. It sounds too harsh. There is no music in it. You say it grates upon the ear. But think when it grates upon the soul, the conscience, and the ear, and not by sound only, but a dread reality when there can be no respite, no cessation, no deliverance, no hope! . . . There was an hour when conscience spake; but you stopped your ears and would not hear. There was a time when reason and judgment whispered; but you soon drowned their cry by calling in some aid against your own soul. To judgment and reason you have opposed *will* and *wit*, and said '*in hell*' was only *in the grave.* In this vain citadel, in this frail house of sand, you will build, until the last seal is broken, the last trump will sound, the last woe be pronounced, and the last vial be poured upon the earth. Then, impenitent man or woman, you will awake in everlasting woe!" [1]

[1] Ninth lecture.

Horrible words, that struck cold terror to the hearts of his followers!

"Sinners in scores are pleading for mercy," so said "The Midnight Cry" of October 12th, and even the most unimaginative must feel the vibrations of fear sweeping up through the intervening years from the deluded ones who believed in the prophecy.

The "History of Philadelphia" (Sharp & Wescott) gives one of the most graphic descriptions of the final days, and we therefore insert it here:

"Fire was to destroy the earth in October, 1844. The excitement in Philadelphia had been growing for two or more years, and by the summer of 1844 it was indescribable. The Millerite Church was on Julianna Street, between Wood and Callowhill, and there Miller's followers met night and day, and watched the stars and sun, and prayed and warned the unrepentant that the 'Day of Judgment was at hand.'

"Many of them began to sell their houses at prices which were merely nominal. Others gave away their personal effects, shut up their business, or vacated their houses. On a store on Fifth Street, above Chestnut, was a placard which read thus:

"'This shop is closed in honor of the King of Kings who will appear about the 20th of October. Get ready friends to crown Him Lord of all.' ... People laboring under the excitement went mad.

"On one occasion all the windows of a meeting-house were surrounded at night by a crowd of young fellows, and at a given signal the darkness and gloom were made lurid by flaming torches, and the air resounded with the roar of firecrackers. The Saints inside went wild with terror, for they thought the fiery whirlwind was come.

"The Sunday before the final day was an eventful one. The Julianna Street Chapel was crowded. A mob of unbelievers on the pavements stoned the windows and hooted at the worshippers. The police of Northern Liberties, and Spring Garden, and a sheriff's posse, headed by Morton McMichael, were on hand to quell the threatened disturbance. The members of the congregation repaired to their homes, and after, in many cases, leaving their doors and windows open, and giving away their furniture, set out for the suburban districts. A large number went over into New Jersey, but their chief party assembled in Isaac Yocomb's field on the Darby Road, three miles and a half from the Market Street bridge. While here a furious hurricane strengthened the faith of the Millerites and struck awful terror to the souls of the timid. It swept over the city, destroying shipping and demolishing houses. . . .

"The crowd at Darby was gathered in two tents, but so great was it that the children for two days were obliged to run about the fields, exposed to the pelting of a pitiless storm, and crying for their parents. The parents, clad in their white ascension robes, were almost exhausted for want of food, slept on the cold wet ground, and prayed and hymned and groaned incessantly.

"At midnight on the 22d, the Bridegroom was to come, and a rain of fire was to descend from the heavens, and the Saints were to be gathered up in a whirlwind. There they stood on that black, tempestuous October night, shivering with cold and fear — their faces upturned, and every eye strained to catch a beam of the awful light piercing the clouds. The morning broke, and with it came the end of the delusion. The assemblage dispersed in despair, and slunk away silently and downcast to their houses."

All through the Eastern States as well as South and West scenes similar in substance to the foregoing took place. Everywhere bands of deluded men and women congregated and awaited the sound of the dread trumpet call.

The writer received the following letter which brings up a picture of them in the old town of Lunenburg, in western Massachusetts:

"I spent Thanksgiving in Hollis, New Hampshire, and just by chance my eye rested on your notice in the weekly paper — the 'Hollis Homestead' — asking for information about the Millerites.

"What memories it awakened! It took me back to my childhood days, when I listened to my father's telling of what he had seen and known of that sect.

"More than once they were prepared for the Second Coming. They rose in the night, clothed themselves in white, and prayed loud and earnestly that they might be found ready for the coming of their Lord, whom they expected was to come in clouds of glory.

"Once, I remember, their leader gathered them together and went to the hill-top, thinking to be nearer the Lord coming from the sky attended with saints and angels and the blowing of trumpets, to take them into the Heavenly glory. *Such a picture!* — these poor mortals arrayed in white, praying and singing and looking for the Coming, according to the Bible tale. What a literal translation of the wonderful story, from what we of to-day believe in — the daily coming of our Lord by the still small voice, and the other ways by which he enters our hearts and minds!"

In his "Reminiscences," Daniel M. Treadwell describes in a few words the final outcome of the prophecy at Hempstead, Long Island:

"On March 22d, 1844," he states, "the Millerites, clad in their ascension robes, gathered on hill-tops, looking vainly for the coming of Christ from the east. It was a pathetic company, and much of the pathetic quality attended the delusion, in the course of which the more feeble minds became deranged, and not a few committed suicide."

An entry in the diary of the author's grandfather, Mr. George Peabody, of Salem, Massachusetts, dated October 22, 1844, reads thus:

"This is an important day to the Millerites, who believe that the end of all things is to take place to-day. Many are so well satisfied of the fact as to neglect their property, and others have distributed it among their neighbors. The delusion has brought great distress upon the families of the infatuated — and much more will result from it."

An incident which he was fond of retailing seems worth inserting here.

His home was what is now the Salem Club House on Washington Square, and the day before the predicted end of the world he was sitting conversing with his wife and one of his daughters when the maid came to the door and announced in rather a startled voice that Mr. —— was downstairs and especially desired to see Mr. Peabody, — "and," she added mysteriously, "he's got his Sunday best on and acts nervous!"

Mr. Peabody went downstairs, and those left behind heard the sound of a very eager conversation coming up from below. When Mr. Peabody returned, his face showed both amusement and distress, for his heart was a very kindly one and he was truly sorry for the victims of so pitiful a delusion, and he related what had happened.

It appears that when he greeted his visitor, the latter exclaimed, "*Mr. Peabody! — Mr. Peabody! dear sir!* — listen; to-morrow the world is coming to an end! — I've come to warn you! My wife and I believe in the prophecy, but my son doesn't, he's obdurate. I've given away my property to him, as we'll not need it any more. Mr. Peabody — you and Mrs. Peabody have been kind to me — you are good people — I hate to think of you and Mrs. Peabody and your children burning in hell-fire — I do — *truly I do!*"

Mr. Peabody tried to reassure him, and said plainly that he did not feel that they must of necessity come to such a direful end, but he found it impossible to pacify him. Having a good deal of curiosity to know what plans the poor man had made toward meeting the fateful cataclysm, the latter assured him that as far as he and his wife were concerned everything was ready — their white robes were waiting to be put on, and they intended to go up on to the roof of the house and from there await the end. Here he quoted as a justification of this decision, "He that is upon the house-tops, let him not come down," which he considered an intimation that the roof was where they'd best be.

Seeing that his listener was not convinced, he left the house sorrowfully deploring the approaching doom of this good gentleman and that of his family.

In telling about it, Mr. Peabody used to say, "Poor soul! Poor soul! it was pitiful!" — and when the prophecy failed, and he found that Mr. —— and his wife were destitute, the son having refused to give back the property, he kept track of them for many years and saw to it that they did not die of want. He always maintained that apart from this delusion Mr. —— was a normal and perfectly sensible man, and deserved a better fate.

A large band of Salem Millerites marched in white robes to Gallows Hill where the witches were hanged, and watched from that elevation for the signs of the coming end.

Mr. Henry Clair, of New Bedford, whose mother and father were followers of Prophet Miller, sent the author (in 1921) a graphic account of his experience as a child on the fateful night:

"The time was set to take place at midnight," he states. "The eventful day at last arrived. The forenoon passed away and the dinner hour arrived, but none of the elder ones ate much food. Soon after dinner the elder ones were very quiet and solemn — nothing above a whisper could be heard. The children noticed the elders go to the doors and windows and cast anxious looks at the sky, and they thought that something terrible was about to happen, and they kept hold of their mother's dress and hands.

"The supper hour arrived, but none of the elders would eat (the final hour was near at hand.)

"After the children had eaten what their scared natures would satisfy, the members of the household gathered together for a series of prayers, and occasionally some one would go to the door or windows and see if they could see any sign of the event.

"About nine o'clock my mother's father put on his ascension robe and sat at the window so as to be all ready to ascend up. Everything was quiet, and nothing could be heard but the beating of our hearts.

"Occasionally some one would go to the window and look up at the sky, and glance at the clock to see how near the time was before the last moment had arrived. The final moment at last arrived, with no signs of the end.

"Then some of the elder ones ventured to the door, opened it very cautiously and peeked out, and as they saw nothing unusual going on they took fresh courage and went out, and walked around the house and went in again, and held a consultation about the affair, and came to the conclusion that William Miller had made a slight mistake in the time. My mother's father sat near the window with his ascension robe on until three o'clock in the morning (three hours after the time expired), then got up and went about his daily affairs."

Another account of the suspense suffered in awaiting the end is given by Mrs. Ellen G. T. Wood, of Springfield, Massachusetts.

"I have often heard my parents relate the following: My mother, whose home was in New Haven, Connecticut, was one of five sisters (all were quite young). Aside from the family was a young American girl who assisted my grandmother (in those days there was no foreign help), and the maid was made one of the family. My grandfather was quite interested, though not a follower. . . .

"The night of the day appointed by the Millerites to ascend, about eight o'clock church bells began ringing; the sky was completely covered with a brilliant red, the ground was covered with snow, the outlook was fantastic and weird, and without a doubt many were inclined to have some belief in Mr. Miller.

"My grandfather, without saying much to alarm the children, proposed going out to investigate. The children were frightened, and begged their parents to take them. Thinking it best to have them all together, the family went out, children clinging to their parents.

"The maid a short time before had had a set of false teeth made, and as they bothered somewhat she would relieve her gums by taking them out, which at that time she had done, and they were lying on the kitchen table.

"For an hour, after much surprise, the redness of the sky subdued, and they returned to their home, while my grandfather ventured a short distance from his house, where he met with those who had found out the cause was a large fire about five miles from New Haven, in a suburban place called Westfield.

"The maid during this time was quite hysterical. After the excitement was over, she said to my grandmother: 'Mrs. G——, do you know *I left my teeth on the kitchen table!* and what do you think the Lord would have said to appear before him *without teeth?*'"

Mr. John Whitcomb, of Lunenburg, Massachusetts, who gave an account of going to the camp-meeting at Fitchburg, also wrote to the author a short account of the last day:

"I lived in Wells, Maine, and I remember the time they were to go up. Some of them had farms, and they gave them away to any one who would take them, and some left everything, and bid friends good-bye, saying — 'We don't see you any more!'

"They came from far and near to our town so as to be near one another when the Lord called. So the day came, and they all sat waiting — some with their robes on.

"One old lady sat almost a week with her robe on and she said she guessed the Lord had forgotten them!

"One of our neighbors said to my mother: 'Oh, Mrs. Whitcomb, aren't you afraid to have the day come?' Mother said, 'No, don't you care, Mrs. Cain — the world is not coming to an end yet.'"

Mr. Frank Stevens, of Stow, Massachusetts, gave the author the benefit of his recollections of what happened to him in that quaint old New England village as the time of the end approached. He had an uncle and aunt who were ardent followers of Prophet Miller. Mr. Stevens, who was a small boy at the time, remembers the day before the expected end when this same uncle and aunt arrived in a buggy in a state of hysterical excitement. They cried out to his father and mother, "Oh, Moses! Oh, Maria! The world is coming to an end!" — and they ran into the house, and in and out of all the rooms as though they were distraught.

His father was a hard-headed Yankee and not easily influenced, and he told them plainly what he thought of them — and in no mild language either — so they left him alone as one hopelessly lost, and turned their attention to his mother. She, however, refused to be moved by their assertions and exhortations and told them they were behaving like a pair of lunatics.

Mr. Stevens said he distinctly remembered the buggy

driving into the barnyard, and his aunt, who was very stout, getting out and running up the path to the house, calling out and gesticulating like a madwoman; and she struck her feet so heavily upon the ground as she ran that she trod right upon a half-grown chicken and killed it!

While great numbers of Millerites sought the hill-tops as the most fitting place to await the end, many sought the graveyards where friends were buried, so as to join them as they arose from their earthly resting-places and ascend with them. The emotion caused by the expectation of seeing the dead arise resulted in demonstrations of abnormal excitement. Miss Julia M. Warner, of Philadelphia, wrote the author some of her father's recollections of this period of which the following is an extract:

"Father was on a visit to his aunt, who lived in New London, Connecticut, when the last great day was due to arrive. In the early evening, just before actual darkness, they started for the oldest burying-ground to see what would happen. They found a big crowd there evidently for the same purpose, though only a few Millerites. Father said it was great fun for little boys like himself to see grown men and women wrapped in yards and yards of white cloth or sheets, screaming, or singing, or praying, or else rolling on the grass 'same as a dog does in a fit.'

"When the appointed hour arrived for the world to end, there was great silence over all. The people waited and waited. . . ."

Mrs. Ellen M. Davenport, of Worcester, also contributes some of her father's recollections, of which this is one:

"My father was born and brought up in Portland, Maine,

and in 1843 he was twenty-four years old and remembered the great excitement. He was present at the following grave-yard meeting, though not a sympathizer. A great company of men and women made their ascension robes and marched singing through the streets to the Eastern Cemetery, where they believed the dead were to rise. One man kneeled on his first wife's grave, saying, 'Here will I stay till I meet my be-loved, and ascend with her,' which so incensed his second wife that she refused ever to live with him again, and never did. *She could not forgive him!* . . .

"A heavy thunder-shower added to the scene and the kneeling crowd shouted, 'Come, Lord Jesus — come quickly!' and refused to rise even when drenched with rain. One woman shouted, 'I see his face!' . . .

"As night drew near, some were obliged to go home, but many stayed all night, unwilling to believe the truth. . . ."

Another account of those meeting in graveyards for the ascension is from Mrs. George B. Ladd, of Worcester.

"My mother, eighty-six years old, vividly remembers the Millerites in Wardsboro, Vermont. She was eight years of age at the time. Her mother gathered her five or six children around her and explained the excitement. She says the day exhibited peculiar features — a red light, and something oc-curred like Northern lights in the heavens. Grandmother took them all to the graveyard to see the believers gather there in shrouds, shouting and crying. A woman who had died several days before was kept in her shroud without burial to meet the Lord! Grandfather, as one of the Select-men, went there to protest.

"Mother is unusually observant and we have found her

recollections of her early life invariably correct and shrewd."

The following old Millerite hymn in the collection of "The Millennial Harp," published in 1843 by Joshua V. Himes, was sung at these meetings in graveyards:

> "You will see your Lord a-coming
> While the old Church yards
> Hear the band of Music
> Which is sounding through the air.
>
> "Gabriel sounds his mighty trumpet
> Through the old Church yards,
> While the band of Music
> Shall be sounding through the air.
>
> "He'll awake all the Nations
> From the old Church yards,
> While the band of Music
> Shall be sounding through the air.
>
> "There will be a mighty wailing
> At the old Church yards,
> While the band of Music
> Shall be sounding through the air.
>
> "O Sinner, you will tremble
> At the old Church yards,
> While the band of Music
> Shall be sounding through the air.
>
> "You will flee to rocks and mountains
> From the old Church yards,
> While the band of Music
> Shall be sounding through the air.
>
> "You will see the Saints arising
> From the old Church yards,
> While the band of Music
> Shall be sounding through the air.
> .    .    .    .    .    .    .
>
> "Then we'll shout, our sufferings over,
> From the old Church yards,
> While the band of Music
> Shall be sounding through the air."

# CHAPTER X

## MORE REMINISCENCES

*"When shrivelling like a parched scroll,*
*The flaming heavens together roll,*
*And louder yet and yet more dread,*
*Resounds the trump that wakes the dead!"*

*Millerite hymn*

MOST of the towns and villages in western Massachusetts were hot-beds of Millerism, and each had its own experience while awaiting the end of all things terrestrial.

Westford, perched upon a high ridge of granite boulders, holds a most poignant memory of the last night of the great delusion. Mr. John Fletcher, a member of one of the oldest families there, gave the author a vivid account of it, which he had heard from childhood up from his father, who was not a believer in Prophet Miller's doctrine, but was deeply interested as an onlooker, and was a witness of all that happened to his followers in Westford.

The principal meeting-place of the Millerites there was in a fine old mansion facing the green on the site of which now stands the Fletcher Memorial Library. It was owned by a man named Bancroft, and he and his family were held in high esteem by the townspeople, and it caused much comment that they and a family of Leightons and also one named Richardson, all well-to-do people with a certain amount of education, should have fallen so completely under the spell of the delusion, but they did so with great enthusiasm and faith, and the Bancroft house was filled to overflowing with large numbers of persons as deluded as themselves. Every believer in the prophecy in Westford was an ardent one — there was not a lukewarm soul among them. According to Mr. Fletcher's father, many of them had white robes ready, and each one prayed loud, and sang loud, and shouted loud; and on this last night the unbelievers who were not up to see what was going to happen, lay awake listening to the tumult of sound that issued forth from the Bancroft mansion.

Now there was a man who lived near by who was generally known by the name of "Crazy Amos." He was somewhat addicted to drink and was one of those queer characters sometimes found in country districts. He was the possessor of a very large horn, and it so happened that, as he lay in his bed listening to the sound of voices that rose and fell like the waves of an incoming tide, a sudden thought flashed through his befuddled brain, and jumping out of his bed he hurriedly dressed himself, and seizing his horn he rushed out upon the village green and blew a terrific blast upon it. The poor deluded fanatics, now congregated in the Bancroft house to await the awful summons of the Holy Angel Gabriel, heard the sound and for a moment a death-like stillness came over the assembly; then, uttering a great shout of exaltation, they rushed tumultuously in a body out of the house and on to the green, hustling and jostling each other in a frantic attempt to secure an advantageous position from which they might easily be "caught up into the air."

When they gained the green, they gazed about in bewilderment, scanning the heavens, looking first at the east, then at the north and south, then at the west, and to their astonishment they could see nothing unusual in the night skies.

Then of a sudden came another terrible blast from a horn — loud and clear — awaking the echoes!

With one accord a great shout went up — "*Hallelujah! Hallelujah! Glory! Glory!*" and believing the fulfillment of the prophecy to be at hand they strained their eyes upwards, searching the heavens again, expecting any moment to see the angelic hosts appear, and they raised their arms high above their heads in an attitude of prayer and supplication. Then a regular fanfare rang out, and one of them espied their neighbor "Crazy Amos" blowing as though for dear life upon his horn.

A muffled exclamation of dismay, mixed with anger and resentment, escaped from the lips of the humiliated enthusiasts, who retreated into the house again in dire confusion, exhausted and trembling from the high pitch of ecstasy which they had reached for the space of a few supreme moments, and from the sense of shame at having been so duped, while they clasped their hands over their ears so as to deaden the sound of the gibes and taunts of "Crazy Amos," who shouted after them: "*Fools!* go dig your potatoes — for the Angel Gabriel he won't go a-digging 'em for ye!"

The whole place was stirred over the occurrence. Some slapped their sides and laughed loud over the discomfiture of the deluded Millerites, while others shook their heads, and felt sorry for them, and deplored the act of "Crazy Amos."

The members of the Richardson family had escaped the ignominy that these others had suffered because very early that morning they had gone to Littleton, just a few miles away, so as to ascend with the Hartwell family with whom they were related. Previous to this they had disposed of all their property, giving away all their furniture, cows, farming utensils, and money, believing that they would have no more need of anything belonging to life upon this earth. When they reached the Hartwell house, they found a great concourse of people assembled there and the house full. There were quite a number of children who had accompanied their parents. One of these, now an old man, gave the author an account of what happened.

"At this place of meeting the people were subdued and solemn. The weight of impending judgment hung heavily upon them, causing long periods of silence through which nervous tremors seemed to percolate. The elders held their Bibles in their laps and tried to read, but every now and then they addressed each other in whispers and the children heard them say: 'It will surely come before morning — along in the small hours, maybe'; and they huddled together in corners, their little hearts shrinking in fear. Straw was laid on the floor so that those who wished could lie down and rest. One or two did so, but the majority sat in chairs and on benches, wide awake and on the watch.

"As the night wore on, one by one the children, who became exhausted from the nervous tension, curled themselves up on the floor and sank into a fitful slumber. The elders, noticing this, exchanged glances and raised their eyebrows, but said nothing. They sat motionless — listening — and waiting for the end with beating pulses. . . .

"The next day about noon the Richardson family, utterly disappointed and disillusioned, wended its way home, an impoverished, disheartened little band, their wagon drawn by an old horse as forlorn-looking as themselves.

When they reached a certain point near the top of the hill, from which they could look down upon their farm, they saw two or three of their saner relatives harvesting the crops which had been left untouched because they had truly believed that they would never have any use for them. One kindly neighbor from a near-by town went to all those to whom they had recklessly given their money and begged them to return it to these unfortunate victims of the delusion. Some of them complied with the request, but there were one or two who refused."

A quaint statement made by a convert to the doctrine at a meeting which took place in Springfield at this time will show how they made it an act of faith to abandon their crops.

"In the spring of the year," she boasted, "husband had not seen the light, and planted his crops. But now he has found the Lord, and the weeds are higher than the corn, Glory to God!" [1]

According to Mrs. Rose P. Preston, of Fair Haven, Vermont, many of the rural people in that locality cut down their apple orchards.

At Groton, Massachusetts, the tension was at breaking point. This was the home town of Elder Boutelle, but as he, good man, was running with the message all the time, the leadership was in the hands of Benjamin Hall, a fire-eater in fanaticism, who was ostensibly a follower of William Miller, but who in reality disseminated some theories of his own

[1] Told to Mr. Frederick L. Avery, of Ayer, Massachusetts, by the former Mrs. Eastman, of Springfield, who recalled incidents which happened in that city to her personal knowledge.

THE ONLY REMAINING HOUSE OF THE MILLERITE COMMUNITY AT GROTON

which were wholly at variance with the latter's doctrine, the result being that the confusion of ideas in regard to what was portending was well-nigh distracting to those awaiting the end. Groton had acquired some reputation as a centre of rebellion to orthodox creeds, and a few years before, in 1840, had held a convention of followers of Prophet Miller and Come-Outers. It had attracted the notice of the public and a number of persons went there largely from curiosity, to learn upon what grounds they based their theories, and among others were Theodore Parker, A. Bronson Alcott, George Ripley, of Brook Farm fame, and Christopher P. Cranch, of Newton, who walked there from Concord. Since then the Millerites had far outstripped the Come-Outers in number, and many of the foremost men of the place had succumbed to the delusion that the end of all things was at hand.

The principal building where the Millerite meetings were taking place stood upon the site of what is now the Parents' Club House of Groton School.[1] It was a strange-looking structure divided into two parts — one part for the men and the other for the women. Around the building were scattered houses where the Groton School buildings now stand, and these were all occupied by Millerites, and they were invariably referred to as the "Community."

Mr. Phineas Harrington, of Groton, who was born in 1827, gave the author the following items:

"The Millerites had also a meeting-place left hand going down to Willowdale, and it was called by the 'scoffers' *Pol-*

[1] Saint John's Episcopal School. (Head-Master, the Reverend Endicott Peabody.)

*liwog Chapel*, the land being swampy there. Services were held every Sunday all day, people bringing their food with them. They came in all sorts of conveyances. Oxen dragged a sleigh loaded with people, men, women, and children out for the day, rain or shine.

"Mr. Pulman would send his ox team round to get any one. He had meetings in his own house in West Groton, now occupied by James Hill. They filled all the rooms downstairs. The final day he took his own family out in a field with the ox team. People laughed and said, 'What! going to take them *nice oxen* up there?'"

How ruthless the "scoffers" were, with their gibes and their taunts!

Mrs. Ellen A. Barrows, of Groton, also has memories of those days which reveal the extent of the delusion. She remembers distinctly being sent by her mother to the "Community" a week before the expected end, to try to get a young girl who lived there to come to "help out" with the cooking. "The man who drove the horse," Mrs. Barrows wrote the author, "claimed it was all nonsense to go over there, for they were all getting ready to 'go up,' and making their ascension robes and everything. When I rang the bell a pale, frightened-looking woman came to the door, and in answer to my inquiry if she had a daughter who could come and help my mother, she said: 'I am very sorry, but I have called my daughter home to prepare her soul for the great change that is coming. Time will come to an end and we are going to leave the earth.' I said, 'How are you going?' She replied, 'The Lord will take all the prepared good to heaven, and the world will be destroyed.' I said, 'Can she come over the week after if this doesn't happen?' Young as I was I never forgot the horrified look that came over her face, or the tears that filled her large blue eyes!"

Mrs. L. E. Starr, of Pepperell, gives a quaint account of what happened in her own family.

Her grandfather, Aaron Mason, then lived in the fine old house now known as the Groton Hospital. He was a most ardent follower of Prophet Miller, and upon one of the occasions when the latter lectured in Groton this good man assented so loudly to everything the Prophet said, and repeatedly exclaimed, "Amen!" in such resounding tones, that the boys nicknamed him "Gabriel Mason," because they claimed that the Angel's trumpet would not ring out louder than his voice did in meeting. His wife had some vague doubts, but his daughter was equally convinced of the truth of the prophecy, and Mrs. Lizzie Davis, who had lived in Groton most of her life and is now in the one hundred and third year of her age, made an ascension robe for Aaron Mason's daughter, and also one for the daughter's friend to wear when the Great Moment should arrive. The author has known Mrs. Davis for years, and has talked over the circumstance a number of times with her, and this dear old lady explained to her that "Aaron Mason's daughter had to be satisfied with white cotton cloth that had a little black sprig pattern scattered over it, because all the plain white cloth available there had been sold to others for robes, but," she declared, "you couldn't see the sprigs from a little distance, so it made no odds."

When the day arrived, the Mason family decided to go over to the "Community" in order to go up with their friends, but early in the morning Mrs. Mason, who, though ostensibly a firm believer, still clung to certain elements of caution, said that before going "she guessed she'd bake some bread."

Her husband was exceedingly outraged at the remark and said, there was no use baking bread as long as the world was coming to an end. "Yes," she replied, nodding her head slowly, "but *supposing it doesn't happen?*"

At this suggestion Aaron Mason grew exceedingly wrathful, and then and there forbade her to bake any, "but," said Mrs. Starr, "she did bake some on the sly, and put it in the cupboard, so when they returned next morning she had something to give him for his breakfast, and after the terrible excitement of waiting for the end and it not coming, he was hungry enough for it, goodness knows!"

The inability fully to appreciate the all-inspiring thought of the Day of Judgment was pitiably evident everywhere. The majority of brains could not register it; they were filled with confusion. Prophet Miller and Elder Boutelle and some of the more spiritual of the brethren dwelt with joy and reverence upon the expected Second Coming of the Saviour; but it must be said that in most cases — certainly throughout the rural districts — this expectation was so shrouded in mystery that the destruction of the earth and the evil thereon, and the anticipation of being suddenly caught up into the air with friends and relatives, took precedence over every other consideration. If the experience showed nothing else, it revealed how well-nigh impossible it is for the majority of human minds to divest themselves of material conceptions. Thus Miss Betsy Farnsworth — "Aunt Betsy"

MRS. LIZZIE W. DAVIS, OF GROTON

From a photograph taken on her hundredth birthday, December 26, 1921. She made white ascension robes for Lizzie Mason, of Groton, and for her friend Miss Butterfield, of Lowell, in 1844.

as she was always called in Groton — feeling very much confused by all she had been told in regard to what was about to happen, and exceedingly nervous, declared finally that she was going to be prepared for anything, no matter what, and forthwith invested in an expensive set of bran-new false teeth, made herself a white ascension robe, and when she went to the "Community" in order to go up with the others she carried with her a green silk umbrella, presumably to use as a parachute should the occasion call for it! — the poor soul had given away most of her property, but fortunately recovered it later.

Dear quaint old characters, where could any be found nowadays to react thus ingenuously to the expectation of so overwhelming an experience? It can only be partially equalled by an account given to the author by Miss Marion R. Sawyer, of Rockville, Long Island, who told of an old lady now living with her, whose husband's sister had her home in Edentown, New Jersey, at the time of the great excitement about the approach of the end of the world, and who, having listened to all sorts of speculation as to what in all probability would happen, and heard the views of various self-appointed preachers, but finding little to cling to as a certainty, decided to follow her own notions, and the night before the expected end "she washed her hair with great care, and the next morning put on an entire new outfit of clothing so as to be scrupulously clean, and she spent the entire night praying for her entire family, and that their future life might be almost as a continuation of the life on earth."

These are individual cases, to be sure, but they serve to emphasize the limitations of spiritual vision in even good and conscientious persons.

Different types of minds were differently affected. Some poor souls, hearing much said about being "caught up into the air," and being unable to understand how such a thing could happen, bought big laundry baskets and planned to sit in them when the time came. Miss Lucy C. Hazelton, of Hampton, New Hampshire, corroborates this in a letter to the author. "I am Hampton born," she writes, "and have heard my relations tell of a company of Millerites dressed in white taking baskets along to go up in, and going up Hampton Falls Hill, and remaining there all day." According to this same letter they returned after dark dragging the baskets after them.

It must be remembered that there was good reason for all the confusion of ideas that troubled the minds of so many throughout the country districts. There were no daily papers or free rural deliveries at that time to keep those living in secluded villages or on lonely farms in touch with the big centres of the outside world. A weekly paper or two might find their way to some fortunate individuals, and they in turn passed them on to their neighbors — a slow process of imparting news, at best. At this time, however, every village was flooded with literature announcing the coming end of the world and the theories connected with it, many of which were too involved for the average mind to grapple with; more than that, a general education was not available as it is now, and there were many farmers and their families who could not undertake to decipher the intricacies of King Nebuchadnezzar's dream nor William Miller's interpretation of the prophecies of Daniel — all that they dwelt upon was that the world was coming to an end and so acted according to their mental ability to absorb such an overwhelming thought. The effect of this upon some of the more untrained minds was extraordinary. For instance, Mr. John F. Wilson, of Rutland, Vermont, was personally acquainted with a man who made a pair of wings for himself, "and as the hour approached got up on to the barn and on the stroke of the hour started on his flight which ended on the ground within a few feet of the barn and resulted in a broken leg. This man afterwards became a deacon in an orthodox church and was highly respected in the community when I knew him."

This act of jumping from high places was very prevalent. Mr. George Newhall, of Swampscott, tells of another case. "I remember very well," he writes, "of hearing my mother tell about the encampment on the horse pasture in North Salem, near where we lived in those days. One incident I remember in particular she said which happened at that time. A man by the name of Chase (I knew him well in after years) seemed very much excited and carried away by Millerism. He climbed a tree about thirty feet high and jumped off, and fortunately for him landed on a large clump of barberry bushes which saved his life. I was acquainted with several families of Millerites — one family named Glidden and one named Hambler."

A correspondent from Worcester contributed a still more pitiful yet ludicrous incident showing the condition of the poor warped minds that were at least temporarily unbalanced by the delusion.

"One man," she writes "(I will not use names, as his descendants might not like it), put on *turkey wings*, got up in a tree and prayed that the Lord would take him up. He tried to fly, fell, and broke his arm. . . . I remember well my father and mother talking about it. I remember hearing them say that some went insane over it" [the delusion].

As has been stated further back, statistics show that the Worcester Insane Asylum was full of unfortunate men and women at that time whose minds had given way under the strain of awaiting the summons that would precede the awful destruction of the world.

Through his stepmother who lived in Springfield during this period and who was interested, though not a believer in the prophecy, and witnessed many demonstrations of the feverish excitement existing at that time among the adherents of it, Mr. Frederick L. Avery, of Ayer, Massachusetts, was able to give some interesting facts, having listened to her tell of these many times over, and he cited a case along the same lines as the foregoing which was as follows:

When the appointed day arrived a large number of frightened men and women were led by one of the Elders to a spot halfway up a hill outside the city, and under the influence of an abnormal exaltation he was overcome by this same desire to jump into the air which attacked so many. While they were all tremulously looking for the signs of the coming end, and as time went on and nothing happened, the tension grew very severe. "After a long wait," Mr. Avery states, "the Elder, in a white robe, got up on a big stump, and with arms outstretched jumped skyward — but landed on earth. This delusion," he goes on to say, "resulted in insanity with many."

There is one curious fact in regard to this extraordinary

HOME OF AARON MASON AT GROTON, NOW THE GROTON PRIVATE HOSPITAL, INC.

period which is that the men were even more prone to commit extravagances than the women, who not infrequently believed, but with certain *reservations*. Mrs. Aaron Mason, of Groton, who baked a loaf or two of bread before preparing to ascend, so as to be ready, whichever way things went, was only one of many wives who kept a grain of common sense in the back of their brains, though their husbands had cast theirs to the four winds. There was the wife of Dr. Smith, a dentist in Castleton, Vermont, who exemplified this very clearly. Her husband was a very prominent man there; he owned a large farm, and was also the possessor of a fine herd of cattle. As the autumn came on, he fell a victim to the delusion, and when the appointed time drew near he sat for three days and nights in his front hall with his wife's plaid cloak on awaiting the awful summons. His wife thought a good deal of her cloak, and she hinted to him that when the moment came for him to be "caught up into the air he'd best let the cloak slip from his shoulders!"

We commend her thrift and foresight!

Miss Honora Harrison, aged eighty-nine, and her sister Miss Sarah N. Harrison, aged eighty-six, of Castleton, Vermont, knew Dr. Smith and his wife very well and communicated many things about them to the author, as did also Miss Mary Gerrish Higly whose father knew all about this incident as well as others. But when Mrs. E. H. Parmelee, of Brandon, Vermont, wrote of having met Dr. Smith when he was an old man one Christmas morning and greeted him with a cheerful "I wish you a Merry Christmas," his somewhat startling reply, "You don't know whether the Lord was born on the Fourth of July or not!" makes it permissible to suspect that the fogs of delusion had not wholly cleared from the poor gentleman's brain even then!

It is a curious fact that waves of delusion produce similar impulses irrespective of geographical latitudes and longitudes, and while with Lady Hester Stanhope, the eccentric Englishwoman living in her villa on Mount Lebanon, they took the form of keeping a white Arab horse on which the Lord could enter Jerusalem at his Second Advent, so thousands of miles away, in the little New England town of Castleton, Vermont, they made a white robe for Him to wear when He should come, and Mrs. Catherine (White) Grant, of Leicester, Massachusetts, states that "David Parsons, of Worcester, I have heard my father say, was so certain of the Lord's coming that he had his shay painted, varnished, and refitted, so that the Lord should have it to ride in." And just as the beautiful though eccentric Harriet Livermore climbed a tree on the Mount of Olives and passed a night in the branches, so at a distant point on the globe, at Harvard, Massachusetts, old Mr. Hardy, a most respectable man, but full of rheumatism, managed to clamber up to the very top of an apple tree that stood in the pasture, and passed a most uncomfortable night in it, awaiting the end, and when discovered there by his neighbors the next morning he had become *cast*, as it were, and could move neither hand nor foot, and it took hours to get him down. Mr. Chaffee, the father of Mrs. W. S. Dudley, of Harvard, was one of the neighbors who assisted in the undertaking.

An old lady in New Bedford wrote to the author of a whole family (relatives of hers) who perched on the branches of an apple tree dressed in their white robes for one whole night.

"It passed," she wrote, "and the father and his family came down to earth disillusioned and poverty-stricken, to begin life over again."

In an extract from a paper prepared in connection with the celebration of the one hundred and fiftieth anniversary of the incorporation of the town of Wilbraham, Massachusetts, June 15, 1913, written by Chauncey E. Peck, he says:

"I remember hearing Dr. Abial Bottom, of South Wilbraham, telling my great-uncle, Dr. Gideon Kibbs, of an experience of his while driving along on Main Street toward his home, a little south of the 'Greens.' It was in the early evening, and suddenly his horse stopped, apparently frightened at something he saw up in a tree close at hand. The doctor himself looked and saw a shape resembling a human figure up among the branches, and he asked: 'What are you doing up there at this time of night?' A woman's voice answered substantially: 'Before the morning sun shall rise the fires from heaven will descend and this earth will be melted in the fierce heat. I have on my ascension robe, and am waiting to be wafted to the realms of Light beyond the skies.'

"The sound of the woman's voice relieved the anxiety of the horse, and the doctor drove on to his home without giving any advice."

Such actions seem inconceivable to us in these more enlightened days, yet in all ages there are unfortunate ones who lack the power to keep their mental balance under the stress of great emotions, and to await an event fraught with such terrifying possibilities as the conflagration and complete destruction of the earth which feels so solid beneath our feet, and the sudden coming to judgment was enough to befuddle many a brain that under ordinary circumstances worked with sanity and order. The direful effects were manifest in the young as well as the old; no age was immune to the disintegrating processes produced by this overwhelming anticipation of chaos.

Great numbers of young women at Lowell became subject to these devastating emotions, and Mrs. S. H. Parker, of Pratt's Junction, whose mother lived in Lowell during that period gives the following account of them:

"I well remember mother telling me when I was young," she writes, "about one girl she knew who went out in her ascension robe with many others to the river, after bidding good-bye to those friends who did not get so far as to really think they *must* ascend *then*. Those who were convinced spent much time in singing and praying as hour after hour went by, and at last they felt there had been a mistake, so they sadly meandered their way back to their homes or boarding-places.

"One girl, by the name of Hannah Dodge, boarded where my mother was, and when she and others got to the house, they found the doors fastened when they wished to come in. Some one went to the door and called out, 'Who is there?' Hannah Dodge gave her name. 'Oh, no!' said the one inside. 'It isn't Hannah Dodge — she's gone up!' Every time Hannah asked to be let in the answer came, 'Oh, no — she's gone up!' It seemed rather hard, but Hannah and the others were let in at last."

Many a disillusioned victim of the prophecy was subjected to this same sort of reception when they returned to their homes. In the majority of cases it was a method of

DR. SMITH, OF CASTLETON, VERMONT

inflicting derision that cut the sufferers to the quick. It was not unnatural that those who had to endure the ridicule which followed the disillusionment shrank from their fellow men and grew timid and supersensitive.

Here and there, however, the surprise on the part of those who opened the door for the weary home-comer was genuine. In the general confusion of thought there were some professing to be unbelievers of the prophecy who hid within a lurking sense of uncertainty as to what might or might not happen. For a long time after the wave of this delusion had receded, many of the country folk were wont to refer to this period as "the time when the Millerites went up." There are a number of cases on record of so-called unbelievers in the prophecy running to points of vantage where they might get a view of some especial family of Millerites going up.

Mrs. Caroline F. Austen, of New Bedford, whose childhood was passed on the Island of Nantucket, states that there was a woman there named Meader whom many expected to see go up, and the school children, of whom she was one, gathered about her home in the hope of witnessing her flight. In many quarters optical delusions were prevalent, and Mrs. Elmira Edson Titus, who lived at Claremont, New Hampshire, when a young girl, states that "some of the people there saw angels flying through the air, going in the direction of Woodstock, Vermont."

People viewed the situation and reacted to it according to type. What seemed like an individual case proved to belong to a group, members of which might be separated and at various parts of the earth, or close at hand; the only link between them was unconscious similarity of action. Thus some were impelled to destroy things or to cast from them their most treasured possessions in their last moments of time. In Portland, Maine, as the expected time drew near, according to Mrs. Ellen M. Davenport, of Worcester, whose father remembered all about it, "the women cut off their hair, cut the ruffles from their dresses, threw away and gave away their jewelry, and in fact all their property in some cases." Others broke up all their furniture declaring that there would be no more use for tables or chairs or bedsteads, and they demolished them ruthlessly.

Mrs. Delia E. Dalrymple, of Milbury, Massachusetts, states that her grandfather was a personal friend of a family who split every piece of furniture they owned into kindling wood. Other fanatics threw their belongings into the city streets or out on to the country roads. A shoemaker in New York City was impelled the day before the looked-for end to throw all his boots and shoes and cobbler's tools pell-mell into the street, and the unbelievers in the prophecy made the most of it, all scrambling for whatever they could lay their hands on.

Miss Marion R. Sawyer, of Rockville, Long Island, writes of this occurrence, and states, "To this day we have in our possession one of the shoemaker's hammers which my grandfather, then a little chap, brought home with him."

Mr. Henry Kittredge, of Lowell, who has made an intensive study of the ins and outs of Massachusetts history, gave the author the following anecdote, the truth of which she is in a position to confirm, as she had been previously told it by the late Frank B. Sanborn, familiarly known as the "Sage of Concord," whose death removed one of the last links in the chain of eminent men associated with Emerson, Thoreau, Hawthorne, Channing, Alcott, etc., living in that picturesque and historic town. Having heard this anecdote repeated, Mr. Sanborn one day asked Mr. Emerson if it was true, and the latter admitted with a smile that it was. It is given herein according to Mr. Kittredge's letter dated July 2, 1921:

"A man quite excited, who accepted the belief that the world was to end on that particular day, met in the roads of Concord, Ralph Waldo Emerson and Theodore Parker. They seemed very calm and undisturbed. The Millerite thought it his duty to inform them and warn them of the momentous fact of which they appeared so unconscious. So he walked up to them with an excited manner and said: 'Gentlemen! — do you *know* — do you *realize* that the world is coming to an end to-day?'

"Mr. Parker said: 'It does not concern *me*, for I live in Boston.' And Mr. Emerson said: 'The end of the world does not affect me; I can get along without it.'"

Which goes to show that these serious-minded gentlemen were not without a certain sense of humor.

Another curious phase of the delusion showed itself among certain believers in the prophecy at Harvard, Massachusetts, which is exactly opposed to those who cast away their belongings or neglected their crops. There was a man named Andrew Lawrence who sold his cows at great sacrifice, to be sure, because he said there would be no one to care for them when he had gone up, but he took good care just the same to hold on tightly to the money he received for them, and hoped to take it with him. Another farmer who lived near him almost killed himself trying to get his crops harvested before

October 22d, the predicted last day of earth, and he even hired a number of extra men to help him.

Several sober-minded matrons on Bare Hill, which is part of Harvard, worked until they were nearly worn out in order to get their canning and preserving done as usual. When their mystified and sceptical neighbors asked them why they did this, they replied that their personal view of it was "that God approved of thrifty Christians, and that to leave everything ship-shape would count in their favor."

These are facts that are well known in Harvard, and that go to show the appalling limitations of spiritual understanding that can exist in strong, able-bodied, thrifty, and otherwise sensible men and women.

And while we are recording the effects of the delusion upon the country folk of Harvard, Massachusetts, we must tell about Ben Whitcomb, of Stow, for not only was he a character such as is rarely found outside of a secluded New England village, but he was also a tragic example of the terrible effects the prophecy produced on certain types of mind. The author was fortunate enough to hear his story from those whose memory of him was still vivid and who could give an accurate description of this strange man. Mrs. Annie Page, who lives on top of Boxboro Hill, Miss Sarah Houghton, of Bolton, Mr. Frank Stevens, of Stow, Mr. Jerome Dwennell and his wife, and Mr. Eliphalet Tenney (known to his neighbors as "Life" Tenney) all remember him well.

Ask some of the old people in those parts whether they remember Ben Whitcomb, and they will throw up their hands and exclaim: "*Remember* him? — Well, I guess I do!

BEN WHITCOMB'S HOME AT STOW, MASSACHUSETTS

— Why, he used to scare the life out o' me when I was a child! All the grown folks were scared, too, for miles around!"

The following is an outline of his direful experience:

Ben Whitcomb's brother Jim, having been crossed in love, took to drink and hanged himself. It was after this that Ben lived alone in the old homestead on a lonely tract of land outside the village of Stow, which for some unexplained reason went by the name of Monkey Street.

Now on the road between Stow and West Acton there lived a man who was called by his neighbors "Prophet" Houghton, because he had taken upon himself the task of preaching William Miller's prophecy that the world was coming to an end, and was letting his fine herd of cattle die of starvation because he declared it to be time and money wasted to feed them, as the end was so near, and who in a desire to prove himself to be endowed with supernatural powers stood for one whole day out in his field gazing full into the face of the sun, so he claimed. It was stated, however, by some who saw him standing there that Aunt Martha Houghton went out and held an umbrella over his head a good part of the time which did much to mar the impression he wished to produce. However, he was looked upon as a leader, and his house was a centre for meetings of a most exaggerated and fanatical nature, and it was there that Ben Whitcomb became an ardent convert to Prophet Houghton's rendering of William Miller's prophecy, and lifted up his voice time and again to testify to his belief that the end was near. The excitement and apprehension were more than his overwrought brain could stand, and he became the strange, outlandish creature who is remembered as having terrified the whole countryside.

Ben owned two horses, and after his wits had gone he explained to his friends that he kept one of them in fine shape so that he could enter the Kingdom of Heaven on it when the time came. The other he trained to jump over the highest fences and stone walls, and to deftly clear at a leap the neighbors' hen-houses and woodpiles, and to gallop over potato-patches and through cornfields without injuring them; and though he was liable to be encountered riding over the roads at breakneck speed, shouting out a warning of the impending doom, he more frequently rode across country, clearing all the obstacles in his path as though his horse's hoofs had wings attached to them. Sometimes, to the terror of wayfarers, he would clear the bushes bordering the road, landing right in their midst and scattering them in a panic and with hearts thumping against their breasts, for when he rode he presented a weird and most astonishing appearance, although, according to Eliphalet Tenney, he sat his horse like a general and was a commanding figure to look upon, in spite of his strange attire. Now his attire was so extraordinary as to deserve minute description. It was the marvel of all who beheld it. From his shoulders a flaming scarlet cloak blew out in the wind, covered with what Eliphalet Tenney called "a mess o' gold stars" that glittered in the sunlight. Sometimes it would flow out behind him and sometimes at his sides, but it unfurled itself in great sweeping curves as the wind caught it, like a battle-flag of strange omen.

Old Mrs. Sawin, who lived farther down the road, made

this cloak for Ben Whitcomb during one of her crazy spells. She was subject to bad ones at times when the neighbors had to go in and hold her.

If the cloak was startling, it was no more so than the huge grey hornet's nest which was cut in two and worn on his shoulders like mammoth epaulettes that covered most of his back and chest, giving him the appearance of a great prehistoric crustacean. A collegian's old rusty black mortarboard cap surmounted by a tassel covered his head, with a piece of black cloth sewn to it which was drawn over his ears and under his chin, so that only his gaunt, pallid face was visible. He varied his headgear sometimes by putting the tattered brim of an old straw hat on his head, and placing on top of it the remains of a dilapidated cloth cap which was puckered into a three-cornered affair with long narrow strips of red flannel floating out from each corner, while straight up from his forehead towered a big brush of corn broom, wrenched from some old broomstick. As if this were not enough, bells of all sizes and shapes were sewn all over his clothing, following the seams of his coat and trousers. There were sleigh-bells, cow-bells, a large dinner-bell, and innumerable smaller tinkling bells; more than that, all the old rags he could find he had torn into streamers. These also were sewn all over his clothes as well as ribbons of every length and color and buttons of every description, and on his back, attached by a cord from his neck, hung a goodsized beehive. Sometimes he brandished two unsheathed swords, while at other times he bore aloft, as a flag, one of the Millerite charts made of linen, on which was painted pictures of terrible beasts, and of the ram, the he-goat, and the exceeding great horn, intricately involved in the prophecy.

Surely it was not to be wondered at that when Ben Whitcomb, astride his horse, came galloping at full speed along the road, with his wonderful cloak sweeping and swirling and billowing out behind him, and the beehive jouncing and bouncing up and down, or from side to side, with the bells all jangling, and the rags and ribbons fluttering, and the unsheathed sword-blades flashing, and he shouting that the Day of Doom was at hand, that the school children playing during the recess hour should run pell-mell into the schoolhouse at the sight of him and bar the door, screaming in terror, "Here comes Ben Whitcomb! Here comes Ben Whitcomb! Look out for crazy Ben!" and cower down in a panic of fear lest he should suspect their hiding-place and search them out.

Mr. Jerome Dwennell's wife, who was brought up in Stow, experienced this many times in her childhood, as did also Miss Sarah Houghton at Bolton, and Mrs. Annie Page at Boxboro, for Ben Whitcomb rode over the length and breadth of the countryside.

The people called him *religious-mad*, and to this, strange to say, he readily assented.

"No need o' being scared o' *me*," he would sometimes volunteer confidingly to startled wayfarers he met upon the road; — "I'm just religious-mad, that's all."

To strangers, however, this statement was not always entirely convincing!

But in spite of all these evidences of derangement, Ben Whitcomb had lucid periods when he seemed like other people. He was by nature a kindly man, and sometimes he used

HOME OF ELIPHALET TENNEY

Ben Whitcomb's next-door neighbor, who found him in the woods at Stow

to go to Mrs. Dwennell's home when she was a child, and she would sit upon his knee and listen to the stories he had to tell, and at such times she had no fear of him. It was when he was astride his horse and riding at breakneck speed over the country that he excited alarm.

Sometimes his remarks were singularly to the point. There was a man who lived in his vicinity who was addicted to drink, according to Mr. Tenney, and under the influence of liquor he would go to the barn and cut off the tail of one of his cows, leaving only a stump. After awhile nearly all his cows were denuded of tails, and then it was that he fell ill.

Hearing that his friend was dying, Ben Whitcomb went to see him. He stood looking at him in silence for several moments.

"Well," he said reflectively, "I'll wager you'll not be cutting off cow-tails where you be going!"

And very probably he was right.

Now one very cold evening in February, Ben was seen entering the graveyard. The incident was remarked upon and it aroused a certain amount of curiosity. The next night when the same thing occurred, however, one of the men in the village decided to find out the meaning of it and he crept in there after him. The following morning he interviewed the Selectmen and gave them the appalling information that Ben Whitcomb had managed to remove the stone slab from the Whitcomb family tomb and was passing the nights in it with the thermometer hovering around zero. The very thought of such a thing as this was dumbfounding, and the Selectmen were nonplussed as to how to meet such a contingency, especially as Ben was a large and powerful man and exceedingly set upon having his own way. The matter was under discussion when a sound of horses' hoofs was heard, and a turmoil of excitement immediately broke loose on the village street. People ran out of their houses, gesticulating and expostulating vehemently, and then ran in again as though to get under cover as Ben with his scarlet cloak and all his trappings galloped his horse from one end of the village to the other, and back again, with the new addition of a human skull dangling by a string from his neck, jouncing up and down as he rode, and bumping against the beehive!

Consternation was on every face!

"Don't tell me it's his *father's* skull!" some cried out excitedly.

"Or his *mother's!*" the women suggested, rolling their eyes up in horror.

But Ben Whitcomb divined what they were saying —

"It's my brother Jim's!" he shouted brandishing his swords, whereupon he dug a pair of old cavalry spurs into his horse's flanks and disappeared down the road.

It was useless to speculate upon what was likely to happen next, for Ben Whitcomb's brain took unexpected turns, as every one knew, but it created a sensation when he began to walk in upon the village people at meal-times and place the gruesome relic under the table when they were peacefully eating their pies and doughnuts. Those of timorous disposition were completely unnerved at the sight, and some even went into hysterics. No one dared to interfere with him because he was so strong, but finally the Selectmen, goaded on by public opinion, took a stand. They ordered him to put his brother's skull back where he found it, which he promptly refused to do, but compromised so far as to carry it about in a paper bag, which was an improvement to be sure, but not wholly conducive to a complete sense of security, as one housewife found when she sat down alone in her kitchen to eat her dinner and in walked Ben Whitcomb with the bag under his arm.

"Take away that bag, I tell you!" she screamed at him in terror — "don't you dare come near me with that bag, Ben Whitcomb! — I know well enough what's in it" — and becoming suddenly endowed with strength born of fear she managed to walk him out of the door and promptly slammed it and locked it, and then sat down next the stove and had a good cry.

Finally a day came when the distracted Selectmen were able to lay the poor head where it could continue its long sleep in peace, and Ben looked about for other means of using up surplus energy. He found it when he rode over to a camp-meeting at Sterling with all his trappings on, and there he raised such a commotion that he was taken to the asylum at Worcester.

"No need to get troubled about *me*," he assured them pleasantly when he arrived there — "I'm religious-mad — nothing more." And he behaved so sanely that they sent him back to Stow, declaring that as far as they could see he had diagnosed his own case correctly and that he was harmless. And to this day he haunts the memory of those still living who can remember him appearing and disappearing on the country roads or over the fields, with his flame-colored cloak streaming behind him, and his ribbons and rags and all his outlandish paraphernalia flapping in the wind, still giving his warning that the end of all things was at hand, though William Miller and his prophecy had already passed away and life had continued its course upon this earth unruffled and unchanged.

It was on the morning of March 11, 1877, that Ben Whitcomb, tragic victim of that prophecy, slipped away from earth, leaving only the strange memory of him to show that he had been here. It happened in this way:

He was tired of life, the poor deluded man, and he was growing old, and he was unhappy. Those who saw him reported that he seemed despondent, and they feared that he would pass out the same way his brother James had. There began to be a good deal of talk about it in the village. On the evening of March 10th, three of his neighbors, Jerome Dwennell, Fred Moore, and Eliphalet Tenney, went to his house prepared to stay there until morning, for he had appeared especially downcast that day.

It was a cold, blustering night and the snow was still deep upon the ground. They sat close to the kitchen stove talking in low voices. Ben had been in there with them, and had not questioned them as to why they were there, which surprised them. He had appeared quiet and even cheerful and after a while had left them to go to bed. The three men continued to sit by the stove replenishing it with fuel every now and then as the hours went by and recalling reminiscences of Ben's brother James, and how he was crossed in love and had taken to drink, and then hanged himself; and then of his father and mother and all the family history known in the village. Somewhat after midnight one of them took a light

THE WHITCOMB TOMB, WHERE BEN WHITCOMB LIES, AT STOW, MASSACHUSETTS

and went to the door of his bedroom and opening it gently peered in, and in doing so he uttered an exclamation that brought the others quickly to his side. The room was empty — and the window gaped wide open!

"By Heavens — he's gone!" one of them cried; and they looked at each other abashed.

"The sheet's gone from his bed," exclaimed another in a frightened whisper, and they all glanced at each other again and remained silent for a few moments.

"Maybe 'twere best to take a look in at the barn," suggested the third one nervously, and the others nodded their heads in assent.

Their search was in vain.

Over in the deep woods where the bitter icy blast could not penetrate, Ben Whitcomb had already snapped the delicate cord of life that bound him to earth, and when in the early dawn Eliphalet Tenney found him hanging from the branch of a pine tree his soul had taken its flight to another and happier sphere.

And the village talked it over; and those who knew him best said of him: "Say what you will, there was no harm in Ben Whitcomb — he meant all right — he was just religious-mad."

So they laid him alongside of his brother James in the family tomb in the centre of the old graveyard.

May his soul rest in peace.

"O, there will be mourning, mourning, mourning, mourning,
  Wives and husbands there will part,
  Wives and husbands there will part,
  Wives and husbands there will part,
   Will part to meet no more!

"O, there will be mourning, mourning, mourning, mourning,
        Brothers and sisters there will part,
        Brothers and sisters there will part,
        Brothers and sisters there will part,
            Will part to meet no more!

"O, there will be mourning, mourning, mourning, mourning,
        Friends and neighbors there will part,
        Friends and neighbors there will part,
        Friends and neighbors there will part,
            Will part to meet no more!

"O, there will be mourning, mourning, mourning, mourning,
        Pastors and people there will part,
        Pastors and people there will part,
        Pastors and people there will part,
            Will part to meet no more!

"O, there will be shouting, shouting, shouting, shouting,
        Saints and angels there will meet,
        Saints and angels there will meet,
        Saints and angels there will meet,
            Will meet to part no more!" [1]

[1] Old Millerite hymn, from *The Millennial Harp*, published by Joshua V. Himes.

# CHAPTER XI

## THE STORY OF MARY HARTWELL

"And here we wander in illusions;
Some blessed power deliver us from hence!"

THE following facts and incidents concerning Mary Hartwell and her betrothed lover, Enoch Robertson, during these last days, when the followers of Prophet Miller were looking for the end, were related to the author by a daughter of the late William Boles Willard, a direct descendant of Major Simon Willard, of Revolutionary fame, and a lifelong resident of the little village of Still River that looks across the Nashua Valley in western Massachusetts. Her recollections of this period are very vivid, and as the Hartwells lived close beside the old Boles Willard homestead, the intercourse between the two families was a daily one, and though a child at the time, she watched this romance with an absorbing interest and in after years heard repeated over and over again all the details of it, which were poured into her parents' ears by the mother and father of the heroine of this little tale, besides hearing through them of the account given by the young man himself regarding his distressing experience. Some minor details were secured from equally reliable sources.

There were three daughters in the Hartwell family, but only one of them was beautiful. She was as sweet and gentle in character as she was lovely to look at, and young Enoch

Robertson[1] worshipped the ground she walked on. He was a high-spirited lad; he had even been rather unmanageable until he and Mary plighted their troth and swore to love each other through all eternity. After that he had but one thought day and night — Mary Hartwell — lovely Mary Hartwell!

In spite of the fact that on all sides it was vehemently stated that the world was coming to an end and that the end was near, the banns were published from the pulpit of the little Baptist Church of Still River.

Mary's parents had no patience with those who believed in the prophecy, neither had their neighbor, Boles Willard and his family, nor did the Robertson family give heed to it — they all went about their business harvesting their crops with an inner conviction that they would be planting them again the following spring.

But it takes more than a prophecy to eradicate fundamental qualities from ordinary human nature, and when Enoch's father, who was known to be exceedingly well-to-do, showed himself ready to lavish both money and affection upon his son's future bride, even those who cried loudest that Time was short exhibited their fair share of curiosity as rumors of the preparations that were being made for the wedding leaked out from various members of both families; and when young Robertson not only presented Mary with an engagement ring that outshone any yet seen in Still River, and, as if that were not enough, drew forth from a shiny leather case a beautiful solid gold watch and placed it

[1] Out of regard for descendants, Hartwell and Robertson names are slightly changed from the original at the request of the venerable lady who gave the facts of the story to the author.

THE BOLES WILLARD HOMESTEAD AND THE " HARTWELL " HOME, STILL RIVER, MASSACHUSETTS

in her hands, such extravagance produced a profound impression. Mary's parents, not wishing to be outdone, bought a wedding outfit for her that certainly made a stir in the village. There was a dower chest filled with linen; and the bran-new cowhide trunk, all ready and waiting for the honeymoon, contained all that a bride could wish for wherewith to adorn herself. As for the wedding gown, it was spoken of with bated breath; rumor had it that it was fit for a city bride.

And the young lovers were as happy as the days were long — he ardent and proud of his choice, and she tender and smiling and lovely as a flower. The village looked on indulgently when they walked down the road hand in hand.

But as the wedding day approached, an indescribable change came over Mary Hartwell. The neighbors took note of it and wondered. Some thought she was ill, she looked so pale. Her lover was puzzled and uneasy. Something that he could not define was coming between them. He appealed to her mother to explain it, but she merely said: "'Tis naught, 'tis just a girlish whim — 'twill be all right after the wedding's over," trying thus to comfort him. Sometimes she succeeded, and his confidence returned, but when he sought out Mary and looked searchingly into her face again, he could not blind himself to the change he saw there, and one day he impetuously asked her:

"Is all ready for the wedding, Mary?"

Now whenever the happy day had been mentioned before this, the girl's cheeks would glow and she would look up at him with love-light in her eyes, but on this occasion, to his utter dismay, she turned away.

"There's no hurry," she said, "best wait awhile."

It came to him like a deathblow! They all began to watch her with anxiety.

In the mean time the days were passing, bringing nearer and nearer the great day that, according to Prophet Miller's theories and deductions and mathematical calculations, was to bring Time to an end, and open the heavens for the Second Coming of our Saviour. Many of those who had not heeded the warning before were now thrown into a state of great agitation, and they went to the Willard homestead to talk it over with Boles Willard, he being one of the foremost men in the place and known to have shrewd judgment. The talk often grew loud and vehement on these occasions, and his daughter, then a child, listened to what was said, and would lie awake at night cold with fear and dread of the trumpet that they said would sound from one end of the earth to the other, and of the terrible "nethermost hell" they spoke of so glibly, and of the "burning lake" and the shrieks and groans. Many a time she hid her head under the bedclothes and sobbed, her only comfort being that her father asserted positively that these neighbors were all wrong in what they said, and that no such things were going to happen. More than once she heard them say to her father: "Why, Boles Willard, man, what are you thinking of not to believe the end is at hand? Don't you read your Bible? Haven't you read about Nebuchadnezzar's dream and the prophecies in the Book of Daniel?" To which, to her great comfort, he replied with some show of vehemence: "I do read my Bible, and in it I find that Jesus said, 'Ye know not the day or the hour,' and that's good enough for me!'"

Now it was noticed that whenever these talks took place at the Willard homestead, Mary Hartwell would hurry across the road and listen eagerly to every word that was said. It was also noticed that quite frequently she would disappear and be gone for a number of hours, and when she returned her face would look drawn and white and her eyes would shine with unnatural brilliancy. In dire distress Enoch Robertson sought her parents again.

"What had I best do?" he asked them; "the wedding day's fixed on, and 'twill be here soon, and when I speak of it to Mary and say, 'Mary, our wedding's coming right along,' she turns away and says, 'Wait — we'd best wait.' My heart is sore about it and I'm full o' grief!"

They tried anxiously to pacify him, and again the mother said, "'Tis naught — have patience with her"; but she said it with less confidence than before and he divined that they also were troubled. And indeed they were! There was the wedding gown all ready and waiting; and the chest full of linen, and the finery and fixings for the honeymoon! And they had all cost money — more than they could well afford! But more than these things was the match itself of which they were so proud! And there was the costly engagement ring and the solid gold watch! — gifts such as no other Still River girl had ever received from her betrothed. "What was Mary thinking of?" they asked each other in dismay. "Was she falling a victim to the delusion that the world was coming to an end?" As she said nothing about it, they did not ask her directly as to whether this was what troubled her. Instead of that they began to inveigh against these deluded fanatics who were, as they expressed it, "caus-

ing a deal o' trouble everywhere." They ridiculed their pre-
dictions; they pointed at a number of families living in the
neighborhood of what is now Harvard Depot, declaring
them to be "no better than crazy folks"; they frowned upon
the camp-meetings that were being held on the rocky pasture
of the Whitcomb farm, now known as Beaver Brook Farm,
close to Littleton, from whence, it was rumored, the singing
and shouting could be heard a mile away. They pointed
to the "Community" at Groton, and again cried, *"Crazy
folks! Crazy folks!"* and they actually forbade her going
near the Josiah Withington farm on the road from Harvard
to Stow. "The goings-on there," they said, "from all accounts were something terrible."

This was true, for those still living who remember it say
that no one who was not a believer in the prophecy dared to
go near the place, so terrifying were the shouting and singing
and sometimes the shrieking that could be heard coming
from that lonely spot a long distance off. It was called by
many "the craziest spot in Massachusetts."

When they spoke of these things to Mary, she remained
silent, but each day they saw her face grow paler until she
looked like a frail, delicate flower of the woods, about to
droop and fade.

It so happened that one day they missed her about noon-
time. It had occurred before, but this time, though they
could not wholly explain the reason of it, they were excep-
tionally uneasy. Enoch Robertson, restless and unhappy,
went over to the Hartwell house toward dusk and was told
that she was still absent. He and Mrs. Hartwell were anxiously talking things over in the kitchen when Mary suddenly appeared in the doorway.

THE JOSIAH WITHINGTON FARM

The "craziest spot in Massachusetts."

"Mother! Mother!" she cried. "Brother Hall over to Groton says it's time we trimmed our lamps; he says all things point to the end being near; there'll be a great light blaze out on Wachusett Mountain to give us warning; he claims 'twill be the light of the Spirit, and we'll know it for that when we see it, for the beauty of it'll surpass anything we ever dreamed of. He says the valley'll go up in smoke — the rocks'll be torn right out o' the earth and we'll be caught up with 'em into the air — that is, if we are worthy. Mother! Mother! why don't you hear what I say?"

They were so taken by surprise that at first they could not speak. The expression on the young girl's face transfigured it. She looked like one who had seen a vision.

Her mother caught her breath. "Mary, child! Mary!" she gasped, "don't go believing Benjamin Hall — he don't know what he's talking about — no more do you — saying all those crazy things that ain't so! Why, Mary — it's the wedding day you'd ought to be thinking of, child!"

"*The wedding day!*" — the words came from Mary as though the thought of them filled her with horror. She walked into the kitchen and looked at first one and then the other.

"'Tis no time," she said slowly, "for us to be thinking o' marriage or giving in marriage. We've no more'n time to think of our souls, and what's to become o' them!"

Enoch Robertson flushed to the roots of his hair, and then turned deathly pale. He took two or three steps toward her, but halted suddenly.

"You'd not go back on your word to me, Mary?" he stammered; "you'd surely not do that?" His voice shook in spite of his effort to keep his self-control. He waited a moment. "I'd like an answer," he said, looking right into her face. But she made no answer. It seemed as if she did not hear him.

One of them ran across the road to get Boles Willard. "Come speak to Mary," they urged breathlessly — "She's talking strange!" — and they hurried over to the Hartwell home. But even he failed to make any impression upon her. The delusion had laid its hold upon her, and she was under the spell of it!

It was close upon the eve of her wedding day that Mary Hartwell disappeared. When they first missed her, they said, "She'll come back same as she's done before." But when night came and still she did not return, a terrible fear beset them. Every time a cart was heard passing down the road they ran out of the house.

"Was Mary on the road you come by?" they called to the driver.

"Nay," was invariably the answer — "she weren't anywheres as far as I could see."

It got noised about as night fell that the girl was missing.

After supper most of the men of the village came to the Hartwell home and offered to search the woods, while the women gathered in groups in the road and discussed the situation. "She's looked bad for some time," some agreed. "'Tis strange!" others said, interchanging glances, and shaking their heads — "and the wedding only a few days off! — Could it be she'd tired o' him!" "Nay," said others, "'tis the fear o' the end that's troubled her, poor thing — she couldn't stand the strain o' waiting."

In the mean time young Robertson, with a face drawn and pale with emotion, was preparing to lead the searching party.

"There's the lake," Mary's mother whispered in quavering tones — "and the river, Enoch; best look there. She may have wandered dazed-like and fallen in — the poor child! — Oh, the poor child!"

The fear grew on them all as night settled down upon them.

The search lasted for many days and nights. The whole village, men, women, and even the children, hunted the woods and the borders of the lake, and the river, and even as far as up on the rocky pastures on Oak Hill, but they found no trace of her. Her lover, frantic with grief, ran hither and thither, calling her by name, but he could hear no answer. He visited all the meeting-places of the followers of Prophet Miller and searched the crowds he found gathered there, but Mary was not among them. After a while the village people left off searching.

"'Tis no use," they said; "we've been high and low looking for her — we can't do no more."

But Enoch vowed that he would never give up hope. "I'll search for Mary as long as there's blood in my veins!" he declared feverishly, and he wandered the length and breadth of the Nashua Valley; and in every village he came to — "Have you seen Mary Hartwell, o' Still River?" he would ask eagerly. But it was always the same answer: "Nay — there's been no stranger around." Yet in spite of the prevalent opinion among their neighbors, neither he nor Mary's parents could bring themselves really to believe that Mary was dead. "She's somewhere with those crazy folks," they assured each other in confidence — yet where? Enoch had looked for her high and low and had found no trace of her.

Finally the day came which was to witness the great cataclysm of earth and the wicked inhabitants dwelling upon it. That morning young Robertson, who had passed a sleepless night, hastened to the Hartwell home.

"There's rumors of great excitement in Lowell," he told Mary's mother, "and somehow I feel as though something was drawing me there. If I started now I'd get there by nightfall. I'm thinking Mary, poor girl, hankered to get away from folks who knew her, and maybe she's in Lowell — you can't tell!"

"In Lowell!" exclaimed Mrs. Hartwell doubtingly — "Nay, 'tis too far."

He did not wait to hear more. He almost ran down the road and in a short time was seen driving over the hill in a two-seated wagon.

Night had already descended upon the town. Young Robertson had left his wagon in the livery stable, and was now hunting the highways and byways of Lowell, through narrow alleys and broader streets searching for some clue which would lead him to the hiding-place of his sweetheart. Demonstrations of hysterical excitement were taking place in many quarters. He could hear singing and shouting down by the bridge, and he hurried to the spot with his heart thumping against his breast, elbowed his way through a crowd of men and women in the throes of a great excitement, scanning each face by the flickering light of the lanterns they carried, to see if he could find Mary's among them; but there was no face there that resembled hers. Some in the crowd were singing with intense fervor, their voices strident, revealing the apprehension that mingled with their exalted emotion. Some were pale with fear and clung together nervously, while others seemed beside themselves with joy, but in all their faces Enoch saw a peculiar flash of something not wholly sane. He hurried away with a sickening dread of seeing that same look on the face of the poor deluded girl whom he loved so dearly — if he found her.

He was turning the corner of a large warehouse when a babel of voices struck his ear coming from the top story of the building, where the windows were all thrown wide open. The rooms within were lighted sufficiently for him to see figures of men and women passing to and fro. He stood still looking up, and a sudden suspicion shot through him.

Finding that the door of the building was unlocked, he bounded upstairs, following the direction of the voices.

Never could he forget the scene that confronted him when he reached the top story, so he told Mary's mother afterwards. It was all so contrary to his sense of balance and sanity that he felt dazed by it. He looked about him and saw men and women in pairs or in groups, each sex separate from the other, flitting to and fro as though unable to keep still; singing and shouting one moment, and the next stopping short and listening. Every time they did this a thrill seemed to pass through the crowd; the atmosphere was charged with currents that befuddled the brain, and he was seized with a mad desire to push his way right into the centre of the room and denounce these people who believed in a prophecy so cruelly devastating in its influence that it had robbed him of his betrothed — of his affianced bride — of the beautiful girl who was dearer to him than anything else in the world. He felt incensed — enraged against them! Then he looked at the faces passing before him and his passion died down; they were drawn and wistful, and he found himself wondering how many of them had become separated from their dear ones, expecting eternity without them, just as Mary expected to reach it without him since he could not believe as she did.

Two women passed in front of him.

They, like most of the others, had on white garments that looked more or less like night-dresses, and their hair which hung loose upon their shoulders partially shielded their faces. But the glimpse he had of the one nearest him set his blood rushing through his veins. — *Was it Mary?* He looked again, and then sprang forward and peered into her face. Was it indeed Mary? Was that his lovely Mary Hartwell? He felt his heart contract painfully. How changed she was! Where had those soft, rounded curves of youth gone to? The face before him looked waxen.

"*Mary!*" he cried, in distress, "Mary!" She turned and looked at him and her expression hardly changed. "Mary!" He seized her hand. "Oh, Mary, come away from here — come back home. You'd oughtn't to be in a place like this!"

His voice was full of entreaty and longing. There was no thought of reproach in his heart for her; it was a great wave of pity for her that now swept over him and through him from head to foot. He had never dreamed of finding her like this! The little hand he clasped in his seemed lifeless; he felt no responsive pressure, and it was cold; he put his other hand over it to warm it. *"Mary, won't you speak to me?"*

She looked at him again — her spirit seemed detached and far away — he hardly knew if she had heard him until she spoke in a low, hurried voice: "The end is very near now," she said, as if impatient at the interruption. "If you have come here as a believer in the prophecy, stay here with us, Enoch, but if not — then go — and go quickly, for the trumpet may sound any moment."

The woman with her tried to pull her away from him, but she resisted her long enough to say, with a little gasp between each word: "You know what it means not to believe? — Enoch! — Enoch! — It means the Lake o' Fire and the *nethermost hell!* — Oh, Enoch!"

The blood flew to Enoch's face. "It means nothing o' the sort, Mary!" he retorted in sudden anger. "What you say's blasphemy! God ain't like that. He's full o' mercy and loving kindness — all you folks better be careful, making Him out like that; it's blasphemy, I claim!"

The poor deluded girl's eyes filled with a look of horror at these words, and her woman companion dragged her away from him.

"Don't you listen to him!" she warned her excitedly.

At that moment a man's voice shouted, "Watchman, what of the night?"

There was a sudden silence and every one stood motionless, holding their breath.

A man climbed up some rough wooden steps and pushed

the door of a skylight that opened out on to the roof and thrust his head out, gazing upward at the sky.

"I see a strange light yonder, behind those trees; looks as though something was coming!" he announced to those below.

A woman in the crowd shouted, "Glory! — Glory!" — and a thrill of agitation leapt from heart to heart. The crowd began to surge back and forth when the Elder drew in his head again.

"'Tis nothing — 'tis nothing, Brethren," he called quickly — "I was deceived — 'tis naught but the moon rising!"

At that moment a cry went up from the crowd down on the bridge — they could hear it through the open windows — but it subsided immediately.

(An incident similar to this one happened at Ludlow, Massachusetts.)

"Mary!" Enoch cried imploringly, striding toward her — "don't stay here with these crazy folks! Why, Mary, girl, the world's not coming to an end; it's all a delusion; there's no sense in what these folks say! The sun'll rise same as ever when the dawn comes!"

She turned angrily upon him. "Go away from here," she commanded; "leave me to go up in peace! — I'll not go back with you — I'll have naught to do with an unbeliever!"

Her lover stepped back as though she had struck him. Then he noticed again how wan the lovely face was, and how small and slim her girlish figure looked in its pathetic little ascension robe. Forgetting the affront just received, he came to her side again and touched her on the arm, a sudden thought occurring to him.

"Where's your hat and coat and your dress and all your things, Mary?" he whispered with a sudden sense of shame and pity at these palpable evidences of her complete delusion.

She looked at him with shining and unblinking eyes. "I don't know," she murmured, shaking her head — "I don't remember where I left 'em — it don't matter any more."

"But, Mary," he insisted, "what have you done with the *ring?* — and the *gold watch?*"

"I don't know," she replied after a few moments' pause, as though she were trying to remember — "I don't know what I done with 'em — I'll not need 'em any more now — so it don't matter."

Enoch turned and stumbled down the dark stairway as best he could. He felt as though he were suffocating. What had become of his sweetheart — of the girl who had pledged her love to him? he asked himself despairingly. — The little ghost-like figure upstairs did not seem in any way like his lovely Mary Hartwell.

He felt very miserable and unhappy as he sat down on a doorstep opposite the warehouse in order to keep watch on what was going on there. He was glad of a chance to think things over. In the excitement of finding Mary and the agitation of his encounter with her, he had actually lost sight of the fact that when the night was over and those poor creatures had discovered their error, he must get her to submit to his taking her home; indeed, having witnessed the power of the conviction these people were laboring under, he had unconsciously almost fallen in with the idea that at least *something* must be going to happen before morning; he even found himself looking up at the starry firmament off and on to see if all was well there. But now that he was by himself he became practical again. He began to consider with apprehension the ridicule which those they called "scoffers" would surely hurl at the heads of these poor victims of Prophet Miller's prophecy, and the sudden realization that Mary might be subjected to some such humiliation roused all the ire within him. He was distraught with anxiety.

The hours were passing.

He heard the clocks strike as each one came and went, and when this happened a great silence would fall upon those awaiting the end. Off and on he saw some of the men go out on to the roof and look about, retreating inside again when the singing and praying would be renewed, but it seemed to him now that the voices were beginning to falter, as though exhaustion were setting in. During one of these pauses Enoch crept up the stairs to see what was happening.

The clocks all over the town were striking the hour again and a breeze was rising, bringing with it the peculiar chill that presages the passing of night. When he reached the top landing, he looked in at the door. They were all kneeling now, and the pallor of their upturned faces startled him, making him catch his breath. He looked hurriedly around for Mary — yes, there she was, the poor girl, kneeling upon the rough floor with her slender hands clasped tightly to her breast and her sweet lips quivering. All the love in his

# CHAPTER XII

## THE DEATH OF PROPHET MILLER

"Watchman! tell us of the night,
For the morning seems to dawn.
Traveller, darkness takes its flight;
Doubt and terror are withdrawn!"

THE foregoing accounts of the various ways in which the coming and the passing of the time of the expected end of all things was met, and which were received from authentic sources, must be followed by a short description of the bewilderment of those who were responsible for all this disturbance of mental equilibrium. In his "Life and Experiences" Elder Luther Boutelle gives us a glimpse of what happened:

"The 22d of October passed, making unspeakably sad the faithful and longing ones; but causing the unbelieving and wicked to rejoice. All was still. No 'Advent Herald'; no meetings as formerly. Every one felt lonely, with hardly a desire to speak to any one. Still in the cold world! No deliverance — the Lord not come! No words can express the feelings of disappointment of a true Adventist then. Those only who experienced it can enter into the subject as it was. It was a humiliating thing, and we all felt it alike. All were silent, save to inquire, 'Where are we?' and 'What next?' All were housed and searching their Bibles to learn what to do. In some few places they soon began to come together to watch for some development of light relative to our disappointment.

"Not quite content with being housed, after such stirring times, I went to Boston. Found the 'Advent Herald' office closed, and all still. I next went to New Bedford. Found the Brethren in a confused state. Had a few meetings; comforted those who came as best I could, telling them to hold fast, for I believed there would be good come out of this matter. Returning from New Bedford to Boston, I found the office of our 'Herald' open, and Brother Bliss in charge there. He said he had hardly been from his house since the time passed. He inquired if there were any meetings being held. I told him there was to be one in the city that evening, and that in other places they were coming together to comfort one another."

But as was to be expected, the moment they began to talk things over, controversies began. The prophecy having failed utterly and completely, reproaches, denials, even accusations, passed between the various leaders of the doctrine, and while the public was letting loose its shafts of ridicule and sarcasm over the position in which these unhappy brethren found themselves, they floundered about in a quagmire of explanations and refutations, sinking deeper and deeper as they tried to extricate themselves from their dilemma. Elder Joshua V. Himes, who could not bear the humiliation of ridicule, swung right about-face, contradicting in bold fashion and even denying exhortations which he had delivered with passionate fervor before the expected end. Thus, in "The Midnight Cry" of November 5, 1844, in an attempt to quell the outbursts of public indignation over the hysterical fanaticism which was so widespread as a result of the preaching which thousands had been listening to, he as-

ELDER LUTHER BOUTELLE

serts that, "although in this late movement many have left their secular callings, yet it is well known that this course has been contrary to our whole advice and teachings while we have engaged in this cause." Yet it was he who just before the expected end, as editor of "The Midnight Cry," had published Brother George Storrs's public confession in which were these words: "I confess that I have been led into error and therefore have led others astray, in advising Advent believers to leave business entirely and attend meetings only." It will be remembered also how strongly he finally came out for the tenth day of the seventh month in an article that teemed with seeming confidence in this new date, but now, to the astonishment of the rank and file of the followers, whom he had assisted in reaching a condition of hysteria, he asserts in "The Morning Watch" of February 20th, four months later, that "the cry of the seventh month was a *local* and *partial* one. It was confined to this *country*," and he goes on to say that the cry produced no effect in Europe whatsoever. He even tried to lay the blame of the origin of the seventh month theory on a man in Philadelphia named Gorgas, who he said pretended to be inspired to give the precise hour of the Lord's Advent; and in "The Morning Watch" of February 27th, which was the new name for "The Midnight Cry," and of which he was editor, he had the temerity to give a solemn warning; "Firstly, of giving heed to the *theories*, *speculations*, and *strained interpretations* of the Scripture."

"Facts which have occurred in our history," he goes on to say, "show that when these theories fail, those who have entertained them are injured as must always be the case when we hold an error instead of truth" — and he quotes from the Scriptures: "For there shall arise false Christs and *false prophets*, and shall show great signs and wonders, insomuch that if it were possible they shall deceive the very elect."

Is it to be wondered at that many of the followers, especially those who were now deprived of their earthly belongings because of having been brought to believe that the end of all things was at hand, should have resented this, as coming from one who had been foremost in promulgating "theories, speculations, and strained interpretations of the Scriptures" among them?

Too ill and decrepit to write out the explanation of the failure of the prophecy which the public demanded of him, poor old Prophet Miller dictated to Elder Bliss a long explanation which he called his "Apology and Defence," and it was published by Elder Himes in Boston. In this he tried to explain how it happened that he finally endorsed the date of October 22d as the day on which the end would come, after having held out against it for so long. He states that he "had no fellowship with the movement until about two or three weeks previous to the 22d of October, when, seeing it had *obtained such prevalence*, and considering it was at a *probable* point of time, I was *persuaded* that it was the work of God." In other words, the old man was swept into the whirlpool of the delusion which had originally generated itself in his own brain, and was swamped with the rest of the victims of the prophecy in a paroxysm of hysteria. At least he was honest in his statement. But he could not resist casting an invective at all the self-appointed preachers of his doctrine, in a letter addressed to "The Brethren," and which was published in the "Advent Herald" of December 3, 1844. In this he says: "The causes which required God's chastening hand upon us were, in my humble opinion, Pride, Fanaticism, and Sectarianism."

"Pride," he writes, "worked in many ways. We were seeking the honors or applause of men more than of God. We were some of us seeking to be leaders, instead of being servants, boasting too much of our doing."

In regard to the fanaticism which had been running riot he wrote:

"I know our enemies accused us of this before we were guilty; but this did not excuse us for running into it. . . .

"Sometimes our meetings were distinguished by noise and confusion, and — forgive me, Brethren, if I express myself too strongly — it appeared to me more like *Babel* than a solemn assembly of penitents bowing in humble reverence before a holy God! I have often obtained more evidence of inward piety from a kindling eye, a wet cheek, and a choked utterance than from all the noise in Christendom."

In the midst of all the endless and futile explanations, refutations, and retaliations that were causing dire confusion and bitterness of spirit among the followers of Prophet Miller, it was Brother George Storrs who, suddenly awakening from his delusion when the prophecy failed, put the whole experience into a nutshell by coming out with the flat-footed statement that he believed *Mesmerism* to have been at the root of it from start to finish!

An uproar of indignation burst forth from those who continued to hold to the doctrine, but he refused to swerve from his newly acquired conviction. The fact that he had been one of the chief advocates of the tenth day of the seventh month theory, and had been instrumental in converting Prophet Miller to it, added to the resentment and bewilderment which this unexpected statement aroused among his associates. But the more they resented it, the more positively he asserted it.

In "The Morning Watch" of February 20th (1845) he states the case plainly and according to the principles of modern psychology:

In reference to some things in the tenth-day excitement he writes, "It was nothing but *Mesmerism*, by which I mean it was the product of a mere human influence; in other words, it was not of God; and I would not say it was of the Devil; hence I must say it was of ourselves — a mere human influence called Mesmerism.

"What is Mesmerism? It is the influence which one body, or person, has over another to act upon them to produce certain results. In other words, it is a mere *human influence*. In itself it is not evil. It is essential to Society, and may be used to bless mankind when it is directed by the Word and Spirit of God, but when directed by one's own fancy, or left to run unguided by the understanding, or judgment, or reason, it leads astray.

"The great point which gave power to that movement was the *positiveness* with which we cried, 'The Lord will come in the clouds of heaven' on the tenth day of the seventh month. Take away the positiveness and the event which that positiveness referred to, and no one believes the excitement that existed would have come into being. Now,

ELDER GEORGE STORRS

then, was that positiveness that that event would come *at that time*, of God? I dare not say it was, any more than I dare charge the Holy Spirit with *falsehood*. The event did *not* occur. . . .

"As the event did not occur, we were mistaken in supposing that we were actuated by the Holy Spirit in making the cry we did in respect to the *manner* and the *time*. I repeat it, it was not of God. I am not disposed to say it was of the Devil; and there is but one other source to which it can be attributed; and hence the mildest expression I could use was to say, it was mere human influence, or Mesmerism. . . . Every day confirms me more and more that it is a true word, and the fanaticism that is breaking out almost continually in some form among those who still persist that the entire movement, about the tenth day, was *all of God* serves to add to my conviction that we were deluded by a mere human influence, which we mistook for the Spirit of God. . . . May the Lord forgive us all wherein we have erred, or gone astray, and help us to be humble and possess Christian meekness for time to come.

"To all it may concern this is addressed in love.

"GEORGE STORRS."

No words can express the amazement and the utter consternation that this change of faith produced upon the unhappy followers of Prophet Miller. Staggered at hearing such an opinion expressed by one of the chief instigators of the tenth day of the seventh month movement, they protested loudly against such a declaration regarding the great emotions under which they had been swayed, but as each denunciation and remonstrance was flung back at him Brother Storrs retorted with disconcerting directness.

"It is a truth that God has declared, 'When a prophet speaketh in the name of the Lord, if the thing follows not nor comes to pass, that is the thing which the Lord *hath not spoken!*'

"Hence it is a *truth* that the tenth-day cry was not of the Lord. And hence also to attribute that cry to the Spirit of the Lord looks very much like sinning against the Spirit!" And as though his restored equilibrium stirred in him an uncontrollable desire to bring matters down to an uncompromising common-sense level, he fairly took the breath away from his former friends by declaring in the same article which appeared in "The Morning Watch" of February 20, 1845, of which Elder Himes was the publisher: "I might enter into details and demonstrate, as can easily be done, that *those who least suspect themselves* have acted under a mere human influence — but I forbear!"

Such a thrust, so evidently aimed at their leader, confused and startled those who still remained under the spell of delusion, and "The Morning Watch" of that whole period rings with remonstrances and controversies — all speaking out their minds.

The followers of Prophet Miller were now falling from the ranks by the thousands,[1] some of them being so shattered by

[1] It has been estimated that the number of sincere and genuine Millerites numbered 50,000, but added to that were hosts of followers who tentatively believed, and followed the real believers in a state of terrified uncertainty. They were as loud in their expressions of conviction as any, but when the end failed to come they dropped away, denying ever having taken any part in the movement. There were also great numbers who became followers mainly from a love of excitement, who attended all the meetings taking place in their

the excitement through which they had passed that in the reaction that followed they became atheists, and stamped their feet upon the ground and denounced the things of the Spirit; while by the same laws of action and reaction many of those still deluded went to even greater lengths of fanaticism, losing all sense of proportion and sane reasoning. A little group, though dazed and almost overwhelmed by the gibes and taunts of the relentless world, remained faithful to to the tenets of Prophet Miller's doctrine, but even they were continually changing and modifying certain points in it to meet the situation.

There certainly were many things happening to disconcert even the most loyal. As an example the case of Sister Mathewson caused many to pause. Upon a general inquiry as to the final ending of her case, "The Morning Watch" of March 20, 1845, states: "We answer that Sister Mathewson has gone the way of all the earth. She died about two months ago. It is well known that she often declared that she should live until the Saviour came."

But the following month Elder Himes writes a letter, on April 11th, which he publishes, to this effect: "Brother Mathewson informs me that we were mistaken about the death of his sister. It was also an error that she said she would live until the Advent. This was *inferred* from some of her remarks by those who visited her. She is yet living, but is quite feeble. She takes now sufficient for her support."

neighborhood, and up to the end did their full share of spreading fanaticism right and left. The imminent approach of Doom did not concern these so much as the morbid and, to them, pleasurable excitement of preparing for it.

It was disheartening. Everything upon which they had laid stress seemed suddenly to be turning to dust and ashes!

As for the old Prophet, it is evident that he did not wholly take in the situation. He was worn out and sick in body and distressed in mind, and his flock no longer heeded every word that fell from his lips with the same sense of conviction that had held them before. He seems to have been wholly ignorant of the denials of Elder Himes, and he ignored the charges of Elder Storrs in regard to Mesmeric influences; his mind still dwelt tenaciously upon his fixed idea — the Lord was coming. He would not tarry long. He might come any moment, and must not find them sleeping! And so like a wounded old soldier he girded up his loins again and, calling for the assistance of one of his brethren, he went forth undaunted to give warning once more, but the worn-out earthly frame was faltering. The bitter discovery that he had lost the power of directing many of those to whom he had once been a prophet and guide, together with the exhaustion of physical infirmities, wrested a cry of complaint from him, and on November 27, 1846, he wrote to Elder Buckley:

"I have not done with *pain*! I have been troubled with headache, teethache, bones-ache, and heartache since you left — but much more of the *last* ache when I think of my once dearly beloved brethren who have, since our disappointment, gone into fanaticism of every kind! . . . And now can you blame me for desiring a hermitage, away from the evil tidings and shameful acts of our friends in this time of severe trial?"

His biographer, Elder Bliss, speaks of this distress of mind and heart as follows: "As his infirmities increased, and strength diminished, he was very much pained by the irregularities, extravagances, and strange notions practised or entertained by those who had departed from his teachings and counsels."

Ignorant of what is now called "mob psychology," he was bewildered at the impotence of his words to quell those mysterious mental currents which they had been the means of accelerating, but which now they could no longer control. In vain he besought his followers not to set any more specific dates for the coming of the Lord; — they would not heed him. It was useless for Elder Himes to reiterate the announcement he published in "The Midnight Cry" of November 7, 1844, after the failure of the prophecy: "The definite time of this event we know not. . . . With our present light we have no revelation of a fixed day or definite time, but we do most fully believe that we should watch and wait. . . ."

It was useless; they would have it their own way now, and make their own prophecies; they shielded themselves as much as possible from the public eye, but among themselves they swerved backwards and forwards, crying first this and then that, trying to find solutions to the questions that beset them.

Some of them in deep and genuine distress of mind began to see flashes of light. "The mistake was in thinking the coming must be in a material instead of a spiritual experience," they cried; and these who suddenly acquired a clearer vision eventually found their way out of the labyrinth of their dilemma on to safe and dry land, but to this opinion the old Prophet would not listen. He longed to see the Lord in the flesh — to hear His voice with his own human ears — to feel the earthly heart within him throb with rapture at the sound. He could not and he would not admit the exclusively spiritual significance of the words he had pondered over so long; it was the material realization of them that he yearned for — the warm touch of the human hand of our blessed Lord, and to see Him dwelling again upon this earth, which though purged by fire would no doubt resemble the earth which he, William Miller, knew and was accustomed to. That was the sum total of his desire. He clung to it, and would not let it go.

But now many changes were noticed in him. He no longer terrified his followers with lurid accounts of hell; he seemed now to wish to impress upon their minds the comforting hope of heaven. All the controversies among them troubled and irritated him. His head felt weary with their questions and speculations. While they were rearranging the tenets of their faith to suit themselves, and quibbling about just what was to be the fate of the wicked, his mind was dwelling upon the peace and joy promised to those who were striving to live righteously.

On September 27, 1847, he wrote to Elder Himes: "The question of the annihilation of the wicked — it has no manner of use to me in this life. And I for one am determined, God being my helper, not to belong to that class in the world to come. I do not wonder that the world calls us insane; for I confess it looks like insanity to me to see religious, candid men spend their time and talents on questions of so little consequence to us here or hereafter."

It was now bruited abroad, not only by the world at large, but by many of his followers, that Prophet Miller's opinions were under the complete dominion of Elder Himes, and this troubled his pride and angered him. According to his biographer, Elder Bliss, he wrote a letter on October 26, 1847, which was published for the benefit of the public and addressed to Elder Himes, which reads as follows: "It has been charged by some that I have been influenced by you and others. Such is not the case. I would say to all that I have never been dictated to by Brother Himes; nor has he to my knowledge ever tried to direct me. But these things do not affect me. I am able to bear all that my enemies can heap upon me, if the Lord helps me."

The world gives no quarter to failures, and the failure of the prophecy naturally subjected William Miller to unmitigated ridicule, but the lowering of his supremacy in the opinion of many who up to his failure regarded his word on Scriptural interpretations as final authority was as bitter a humiliation as anything he had to bear. But how surely retribution comes! He had mocked and ridiculed others for their religious convictions in his youth; it was his turn now to suffer all the pain that he had inflicted, and under the stress of it his health was becoming very noticeably impaired. Then a staggering blow fell upon him. The eyes which had been searching the heavens so long for signs of the Lord's coming were stricken with blindness! It was as if his human sight had to go before he could attain to spiritual vision.

"I have never heard him murmur or say that it was hard. — I think he feels somewhat cast down, but not forsaken." So wrote one of his daughters-in-law regarding this affliction.

Toward the last of April, 1849, his strength began to fail rapidly and in a letter which he dictated to the remnant of his following that met in conference at Boston on May 10th, he said:

"My multiplied and increasing infirmities admonish me that the time of my departure is drawing nigh. My earthly labors have ceased, and I now await the Master's call, to be ready at His appearing, or, if it so please Him for a little while His coming be delayed, to depart to be with Christ, which is far better than to abide in the flesh. I feel that I have but little choice, whether I shall be continued in life till that event, or my spirit be gathered to the spirits of just men made perfect.

"However God may be pleased to deal with me, I am sustained by the blessed assurance that whether I wake or sleep I shall be present with the Lord."

A short account of him given by Elder Robinson, who visited him in December, is as follows:

After describing his approach to the farm he says: "I was welcomed in the simple, hearty, easy style of a Vermont Christian farmer's family. That pleasant, beaming countenance of his wife, and the hearty shake of the hand, told me that I was at home; and the kettle of hominy just taken from the fire was at once prophetic of my supper. And all the members of the family, intelligent, modest, and cordial, made me feel how really glad they were of the call, and to hear from those abroad.

"I was quickly invited into the 'east room,' where 'Father Miller' greeted me. . . . He was much changed, and yet not so changed as to leave all the good outlines of the former acquaintance behind. His sufferings through the summer and fall had been very great. His venerable white locks were few and thin, and his flesh like that of a child. But his voice was full, his memory good, and his intellect strikingly strong and clear, and his patience and resignation re-markable. .... He was sure it could not be long before the coming of the Lord. He wished Him to come soon; but if not, to be taken himself to the Lord."

And so the wandering Prophet — he who had wandered through country roads and city streets, north and south, east and west — had come back blind and shattered to the neat and cared-for home where during all these years his faithful wife, Lucy Miller, had kept the fire burning, and raised eight of the ten children to whom she had given birth. There he lay in his helplessness and seeming defeat. When she looked into the sightless eyes and saw the wasted frame and the brown hair turned to silver, did she recall the young soldier of her youthful days, long since passed?

On the morning of the 17th of December, 1849, they sent for Elder Himes, as they saw the end was near. The man who had brought William Miller out from the rural districts into the turmoil of great thoroughfares, who had pioneered him through the hectic years of delusion and assisted him in giving forth his momentous warning, was the one he called for now. On him he desired his mantle should fall.

A letter from Elder Himes, written in retrospect, gives a short but memorable account of the few words that passed between them.[1]

"On entering the room," he wrote, "he immediately

[1] Sylvester Bliss, *Life of William Miller.*

recognized my voice. He grasped my hand and held it for some time, exclaiming with much earnestness and in a tone of affection, 'Is this Elder Himes? Is it Elder Himes? Oh, is it Elder Himes? I am glad to see you.'

"Then you know me, Father Miller, do you?'

"'Oh, yes, I understand, I know what is passing!'

"He was silent for a few moments, apparently in a deep study. Presently he introduced the subject of my connection with the Advent cause, and spoke of my responsibility; expressed much anxiety about the cause, and alluded to his own departure."

Elder Himes tried to reassure him. "So far as I am concerned," he told him, "I hope for grace to enable me to be *faithful in the ministry I had received.*"

This seemed to comfort him, and he fell into a sort of doze, for he was very weak.

In a few moments he recovered himself. "Elder Himes has come," he said. "I love Elder Himes." Then came another pause.

If he was abandoned by all but a comparatively small following, his own family made up for it in tender solicitude and devotion. He seemed to want to hear the old hymns of his childhood days, and they gathered about him, and at his request sang:

> "There is a land of pure delight,
> Where Saints immortal reign —
> Infinite day excludes the night,
> And pleasures banish pain."

He seemed to find great solace in these words.

Then they sang to him:

> "Happy the spirit released from its clay."

And the weary old man murmured over and over, "Oh, I long to be there!"

In spite of all the ups and downs of his strange life, so wholly given over to proclaiming his prophecy which failed; in spite of the disappointment and all the bitter humiliation he earned as the fruits of his labor, his death was a happy one, and it must be recorded that he met it with the valiant spirit of an old soldier.

He never swerved from his fixed idea, but assured them all with his accustomed positiveness that the Lord was coming, that He was "even nigh unto the door," and on the morning of December 20th they looked at him and then at each other and bowed their heads, for they knew that for him this was true.

It was while his wife and his sons and daughters and Elder Himes were silently watching by his bedside that the summons came.

Like a sentinel on guard at his post, the old Prophet answered. His sightless earthly eyes opened wide and stared into space, but it was with the eyes of his soul that he beheld the all-satisfying vision.

"*Victory!*" he cried out several times — lifting his dying voice — *Victory! Shouting in death!*"

And thus they knew that at last, for him, the blessed Lord had come.[1]

[1] A church was built in Low Hampton, New York, in memory of William Miller.

# CONCLUSION

AND Elder Himes? — that complex character, that indefatigable revivalist — what was his end? Well, after publishing newspapers, tracts, books, and pamphlets full of exhortations to the Brethren to stand firm in their faith and
to continue to watch without ceasing for the signs of the
End for upwards of thirty years, he suddenly renounced the
doctrine which he had been so instrumental in spreading
and took orders as a clergyman of the Episcopal Church.
Without warning he turned the kaleidoscope of Fate and
found himself in a new field, with a new outlook and another
doctrine, the preaching of which opened up new outlets for
his super-nervous energies.

All this happened in 1880, when on January 9th he was
ordained by Bishop Clarkson, of Nebraska, and was assigned
the rectorship of St. Andrew's Church, in the little town of
Elk Point, South Dakota, which even in 1900, when the
last census was taken, then boasted of only 1081 inhabitants.

Through the courtesy of a friend who communicated with
the Reverend Dr. Woodruff, Dean of Calvary Cathedral,
Sioux Falls, South Dakota, who kindly searched the files
for information regarding the former Elder Himes in his new
position as an Episcopal clergyman, the author was able to
secure a few details regarding the end of this versatile man,
which under the circumstances are not without interest.

"I have discovered a unique character," wrote Dean
Woodruff, "but have found nothing of his history before he
came to South Dakota."

So evidently in these new surroundings the Reverend Joshua V. Himes escaped at last from the gibes and ridicule incurred by the failure of the prophecy to which he and the followers of William Miller had been so long subjected.

An extract from an appeal he made to his congregation at the age of eighty-five, in behalf of an effort to build a new church, shows that his energy was still unabated at that advanced age:

"I cannot speak as a young man, for I am old," he declared; "but like Joshua the Son of Nun, with an undimmed eye and vigorous natural force, the best of health, with vigor of body and mind to carry out any work of my mission under the direction of my good Bishop, in what remains of mortal life, I am looking for five years of good work by the permission of the Author and Giver of life, and will then, at ninety, if God so order it, say, 'Now lettest Thou Thy servant depart in peace." He did live those five years and two months over, for he was born May 19, 1805, and died July 27, 1895.

In referring to him after his death in his Convention Address, in 1895, Bishop Hare said of him: "Until a few months before his demise, in his ninety-first year, he still merited the epithet which I applied to him in his eighty-fifth year: 'At eighty-five years of age, he fights the battle of the Church with the gallantry of the stripling David, and preaches the Gospel with the power of a youthful Stephen.'"

He is buried in Mount Pleasant Cemetery, Sioux Falls, South Dakota, instead of in Elk Point, because the cemetery in Sioux Falls is set on a hill, and he asked Bishop Hare to get a lot for him on this elevated spot, "because he wanted to be on the top of a hill when Gabriel blows his trumpet."

So it would seem that in adopting another doctrine some points of the old one yet remained in mind.

But the fact of changing the tenets of his faith did not wholly change his characteristics. At the age of ninety, and only a few months before his death, the Reverend Joshua V. Himes, evidently still smarting at the memory of the ridicule to which he and all the believers in the prophecy were subjected in 1843 and 1844, took up his pen and wrote the following letter, which was published in "The Outlook Magazine" and dated October 29, 1894:

"To the Editors of The Outlook:

"I have been much interested in the articles lately appearing in The Outlook upon the question of Ascension robes. I am glad that public interest has been again aroused upon this topic, for it is time it should be settled, and settled right, and nothing is truly settled until it is settled right. I wish to say that I was intimately associated with William Miller for eleven years, beginning in 1839; that with him I attended hundreds of meetings, laboring with him in public and private, and was with him at his home in the State of New York on the night of the tenth day of the seventh month when we expected the Lord to come; and having a perfect knowledge of everything connected with that work, I *know* the whole story of the Ascension robes to be a concoction of the enemies of the Adventists, begotten of religious prejudices, and that there is not a scintilla of truth in it. No wonder the writer in The Outlook of October

27th did not give his name and address. The statement that 'to be prepared, dressed in their Ascension robes, was the instruction given by their leaders to the rank and file of the Millerites,' is almost too silly to be noticed. The writer originated and with others signed the call for the first Adventist Conference which was held with the Church over which he was pastor (the Chardon Street Baptist Church) in Boston, Massachusetts, in 1840.

"During those eventful days, from 1840 to 1844, and for several years after, I had charge of all their publishing work, and no man, living or dead, knew better what was taught and done by Adventists than I did. There were some excesses such as always attend great religious upheavals, but they were not committed by the instruction of their leaders, and the putting on of Ascension robes was not one of these excesses.

"When these stories first started, and while I was publishing in the interests of the Adventist cause, I kept a standing offer in the paper, of which I was editor, of a large reward for one well-authenticated case where an Ascension robe was worn by those looking for the Lord's return. No such proof has ever been forthcoming. It was always rumor, and nothing more. Absolute evidence never has been furnished. It has always been one of those delightful falsehoods which many people have wanted to believe, and hence its popularity and perpetuity until this present day. I have refuted the story hundreds of times in both the Advent Herald in Boston, Massachusetts, and in The Midnight Cry in New York, which had a circulation of tens of thousands of copies; and no accusers ever made an attempt to defend themselves, although I held my columns open to them to do so. And now, at the age of ninety years, with a full personal experience of those times, before God who is my Judge, and before whose tribunal I must soon appear, I declare again, that the Ascension robe story is a tissue of falsehoods from beginning to end, and I am glad of the opportunity to deny it once more before I die.

"The preparation urged upon 'the rank and file' of those looking for the coming of the Lord was a preparation of heart and life by a confession of Christ, a forsaking of their sins and living a Godly life; and the only robes they were exhorted to put on were the robes of righteousness, obtained by faith in Jesus Christ; garments made white in the blood of the Lamb. Nothing of an outward appearance was ever thought of or mentioned.

"Joshua V. Himes
"Rector of St. Andrew's Episcopal Church
"Elk Point, South Dakota."

Now it must have been his change of faith, or the fact of preaching another doctrine, or his ninety years, that confused the old gentleman's memory in regard to this matter, which seems a very insignificant detail to dwell upon in view of the overpowering magnitude of the subject of the prophecy.

But in justice to the many accounts of the days preceding the expected end that have been gathered together in this volume, the author feels called upon to state that in making so sweeping a statement he widely overstepped the mark. We believe it to be quite true that no orders were issued from *headquarters* — meaning from himself and Prophet

Miller, Elder Bliss, and a small group of preachers associated
with them *from the first*, as to the wearing of white robes, but
there is nothing to justify the statement that they were not
worn by any of the deluded followers of the prophecy, and
there are many still living who can testify to the contrary,
some of whom have done so in this book, who can in no way
be called 'enemies to the Adventists.' Moreover, the author
has diligently searched the files of "The Midnight Cry"
and the "Advent Herald" (the latter covering the years
up to 1860, of which only a few copies were missing), and
has failed to find any reference whatsoever to ascension
robes, or any mention of the reward the old gentleman
speaks of in his letter; nor has she been able to discover the
refutations which he declares he had printed in the columns
of both these papers 'hundreds of times.' There were frequent remonstrances in regard to some other symbolic acts
which were being indulged in, and it is possible that the
memory of these may have caused confusion in his mind,
but the only reference to the very harmless act of wearing
the white robes is in Elder Bliss's "Life of William Miller"
which was published by Elder Himes in 1853, nine years after
the great fiasco of the prophecy, in which it says: "All reports respecting the preparation of ascension robes, etc.,
which are still by many believed, were demonstrated over
and over again to be *false* and *scandalous*. In the investigation of the truth of such, no labor or expense was spared,
and it became morally certain that *no instance of the kind
anywhere occurred*." [1] But Elder Luther Boutelle, a man

---

[1] Letters like the following are certainly sufficiently definite:
"I have heard my mother tell that when she was a girl she remembers that

whose integrity has never been questioned, in writing his "Autobiography," in which he describes the happenings of those days, quotes directly from the very page upon which this statement appears and, continuing down to the paragraph itself, stops short and totally ignores its contents; and why? — because Elder Boutelle knew perfectly well that in his own home town of Groton and in his own State of Massachusetts, especially in the rural districts, to say nothing of other localities, this perfectly innocent bit of symbolism was, if not universally, at least very prevalently, indulged in. Elder Boutelle, like Prophet Miller, was by nature outspoken and direct in thought and speech and free from subterfuge, and while certain of the Brethren, under the sting of humiliation, denied this and denied that after the great fiasco, neither he nor his leader ever belittled the memory of their supreme disappointment by raising or refuting questions of such minor import as the one referred to; their thoughts were wholly occupied with the one all-absorbing hope which, in spite of repeated failure to materialize, they still clung to. In a letter to the author Elder Boutelle's granddaughter declares that to the end of his life of ninety-two years "grandfather was running with the message most of the time!"

"Let the closing scenes of life's drama be spent in the service of our Christ who is soon to appear," he wrote at the end of his "Autobiography," "that we may be able to say

her mother made a white robe, put her house in order, put lamps in the windows and sat up all night waiting for the end of the world to come.

"Trusting this information will be of some value to you, I am

"Very truly yours

"IDA M. WING.

"NEW BEDFORD, *Aug.* 21, 1921."

with the Apostle: 'Whether we live, we live unto the Lord: whether we die, we die unto the Lord: Whether we live or die, therefore, we are the Lord's.'"

Fine old Elder Boutelle! Staunch old Christian! If he was mistaken as to the manner and time of the Coming, no one could question the genuineness of his love of the Master. He lies in the burying-ground in Groton in view of the distant hills which he loved. But he and the others all passed on years ago; all those earnest souls who looked for the destruction of the earth by fire and for the immediate coming of the Lord — Prophet Miller, Elder Bliss, Brother Storrs, and Brother Southard, and the host of Brethren whose voices roused the echoes far and wide with their startling cries of warning — they have all gone; and the Reverend Joshua V. Himes still waits in his grave upon the hill-top for the end which has not yet come.

No more mad Ben Whitcombs gallop through country lanes shouting that the end is near; no more fair maids like lovely Mary Hartwell go fleeing from their betrothed for fear of the wrath to come; no little bands of eager, fear-racked souls go trailing up from village street to hill-top to await the awful summons.

The mysterious wave of agitation has long since receded into the unexplored etheric regions from whence it came; even the memory of it all has almost passed away.

The followers of William Miller claimed that in spite of the failure of his prophecy the whole experience was of God; that through fear of the Awful Day, souls who could not otherwise be reached were brought under subjection and saved from the torments of hell. They forgot the inspiring admonition of the Apostle Paul: "God hath not given us the spirit of fear; but of *love*, and of *power*, and of *a sound mind*."

With this reassuring and illuminating statement to counteract the direful accounts of the strange religious hysteria of 1843 and 1844, and the delusion of William Miller, the book closes.

THE END

# APPENDIX [1]

## SYNOPSIS OF THE THEORY AND CALCULATIONS

Daniel speaks prominently of 2300 days. He has also four numbers, namely, 1260, 1290, 1335 days, and 70 weeks (equal to 490 days).

Each of these days Mr. Miller considers a year: and it is one of his cardinal propositions that in prophecy this method of computations must always be regarded. Accordingly, the 2300 days aforesaid are reckoned as so many years, and are declared to commence with the going forth of the commandment to rebuild Jerusalem, and to extend to the resurrection and end of the world in A.D. 1843; and therefore they are supposed to embrace all the other numbers in the Book of Daniel. The subjoined are the five principal calculations:

### CALCULATION 1

| | |
|---|--:|
| From the date of the commandment to rebuild Jerusalem, B.C. 457, to the crucifixion of Christ, 70 weeks, or 490 years..... | 490 |
| From the crucifixion of Christ to taking away the daily abomination, which is supposed to signify Paganism.............. | 475 |
| From taking away of Pagan rites to setting up the abomination of desolation, or Papal Civil Rule....................... | 30 |
| From setting up of the Papal abomination to the end thereof... | 1260 |
| From taking away of Papal Civil Rule to the first resurrection and the End of the World in 1843....................... | 45 |
| These being added present the sum of the years.............. | 2300 |

### CALCULATION 2

| | |
|---|--:|
| From the full term of the vision as above exemplified........ | 2300 |
| Subtract 70 weeks of years to the crucifixion of Christ........ | 490 |
| | 1810 |
| Add to this the term of our Saviour's life................... | 33 |
| End of the world in................................ A.D. | 1843 |

[1] From *A Complete Refutation of Miller's Theory of the End of the World in 1843*, by Abel C. Thomas. Published 1843.

## CALCULATION 3

From the crucifixion to taking away the daily abomination, the
    second item of the first calculation...................... 475
Add our Saviour's age, 33, and Daniel's number, 1335........ 1368
End of the world in.................................A.D. 1843

---

## CALCULATION 4

For the full term of the vision as before exemplified.......... 2300
Subtract date of the commandment to rebuild Jerusalem ...B.C. 457
End of the world in.................................A.D. 1843

## CALCULATION 5

In Leviticus XXVI, 23–24, the Lord speaks of punishing the
    house of Israel "yet seven times for their sins." Seven times
    (or years) — each day reckoned as a year — 360 multiplied
    by 7.................................................. 2520
Subtract the date of the first captivity in Babylon, at which
    time it is assumed this punishment commenced.........B.C. 677
End of the world in.................................A.D. 1843

Behold how clearly it is shown by four methods of calculation that
the world is doomed to destruction in Anno Domini 1843! The calculation and results will surely be undeniable *if* days in prophecy are
always to be computed as years, and *if* a time signifies 360 years, and
*if* the assumed references are correct, and *if* the dates are all right, and
so on to the end of the chapter of contingences.